BEYOND THE STORM

SALVAGING PHOTOGRAPHS AND PRESERVING
HISTORIES

KRISTA KOWALCZYK

LIBRARY TALES PUBLISHING

Dedicated to those who have survived the unthinkable pain of any natural disaster.

And remembering loved ones I lost as I wrote this book:
Uncle Joe, Big Bill, Aunt Mary, Mark, Bob, Jon, Lyla

There could never be enough photos to contain all of the memories, but holding those special few had a profound impact on me and my writing...

To think that bad selfie could mean so much.

CONTENTS

INTRODUCTION
THE VALUE OF A PHOTOGRAPH

What is the value of a photograph? One photograph can be worth millions of dollars, while another is a seemingly valueless piece of paper. They can be the sole keeper of cherished memories or reminders of the things we want to forget forever. A single photo can be a one-way ticket to success or a life permanently destroyed. They are displayed in homes across the world; they have no boundaries, they speak every language, and they are universally cherished.

A single photograph can have the power to change the future of an entire nation, or it can be of little to no significance, depicting a squirrel in a bird feeder. They can be the most powerful weapon or a calming friend. Their value can change over time too. An ordinary enough photo of second-grade classmates can sit in a box with little thought until, 25 years later, those students reunite and are married. Photographs are in our phones, in our wallets; they are the only thing I can think of that everyone I know has, everyone I know loves, and, as I learned, everyone is devastated by when they lose.

How, then, can that question be answered best? "What is the value of a photograph?" The answer can vary wildly, but it's their power that is without question. There is something about the way a single photograph can impact a person. When an image impacts its viewer, it strikes an emotional response that nothing else in the world can match. I doubt many people go through life thinking about the value of a photograph or even what power it holds. They are so ingrained in our lives that it's almost like breathing. They are ever-present, just quietly being loved, and sometimes even hated.

In a world filled with photographs, there is a special group of people: the ones who appreciate their power most. That has always been me. I imagine it may be you too. We are the keepers of our family history. We are the ones who document a child's first step and a grandparent's long-overdue visit. We have annoyed dads everywhere with "one more picture" or "get together again." Our phones are filled to capacity, and we cringe when we delete even one image. We know right where the box filled with our own childhood memories is stored, and we cherish the treasures hidden in that box. We post pictures, we text pictures, and we feel guilty because we don't print more of our pictures. From the photo holiday card to the obligatory cruise ship or amusement park photos, when there is an opportunity for a photograph, we take it.

I realized, when a family member once said to me, "I didn't take any pictures because I knew you had that covered," that it was officially assumed I would be documenting every special occasion. In my journey to help people with their own photographs, I've learned so much more about that designated person and position. We are a special group. We have given ourselves a job, and with that job comes great responsibility. How will our lives be remembered? What does our family heritage look like? Will our children have a box of treasures like we do, or will they have an overwhelming amount of digital files to sift through? And what is going to happen to that box, to our own childhood? Those images that are already fading today—what will become of them with future generations? What will happen to the box, to the digital files, to the memories?

I have devoted my life and career to photography. Keeping my vast photo collection organized is just part of my daily routine. However, it took Hurricane Ian and an entire community of people with lost or damaged pictures for me to fully understand how rare that is and how few people have adequately secured their own images.

Since Hurricane Ian, nothing about my life has been the same. While there was nothing I could do to fix the devastation caused by the hurricane, I tried my hardest to help and offer some solace to its victims. In the preceding months, I spent hundreds of hours restoring hurricane-damaged photographs. Each person shared stories of catastrophic loss, and with each story came the pain of their lost photographs. They were invaluable, and yet, ironically, most people had done very little to secure them. I found that most people have no idea how to save, store, and digitize the pictures they have. That, or they are overwhelmed by the thousands of photographs they own. After witnessing so much heartbreak and so little knowledge and resources, I knew that this was a problem that needed to be proactively solved.

I can't change anything about what happened, but I can turn that loss into a call to action: for everyone to take the necessary and truly easy steps to get their photographs digitized and properly secured. Since Hurricane Ian, I've poured my heart into that mission, inspiring and helping others to secure their photographs before disaster strikes. Although floodwater was what impacted Southwest Florida, I've since had countless grief-stricken conversations with people all over the world whose photographs were damaged. Each had a unique reason why their pictures were destroyed, but the heartache was always the same. As we journey through this book together, I hope you too will be inspired to secure your own pictures and never have to feel the anguish of losing a treasured photograph.

Let's talk about your photographs

- Have you thought about the most powerful images in your life?
- Has there ever been a photograph that brought you to tears or caused you to erupt in laughter?
- Do you remember a time when a photograph made your jaw

drop or when you couldn't help but shout to the next room, "You have to come see this photo I found!"

- Or those vacation photos that you just couldn't resist sharing with everyone you met for the next six months?
- What significance do these photos hold for you? How much do they truly mean to you?
- And what have you done to secure these images? How are they stored, backed up, and organized?
- Securing these most valued photographs is not a hard task, and it doesn't have to be a mundane one either.
- There are many easy methods to accomplish this. I'll walk you through that process as we go along, giving you the tools and inspiration to be photo-organized!

CHAPTER ONE

BEFORE IAN

Helping people save their hurricane-damaged photos was never part of my plans. In fact, none of the events that led me here are anything I would have planned or even asked for. I had a thriving family and wedding photography business in Southwest Florida. My life was consumed by gorgeous tropical weddings and family photo shoots on the beach. My daily drive would take me across the tiny tropical islands that make up the Sanibel Island Causeway, or have me heading over the sailboat-dotted waterway that separates Fort Myers Beach from the mainland. My commute was like a scene from a postcard, and the destinations I found myself frequenting were the kind of places I dreamt of visiting as a child growing up in rural Pennsylvania. These were places that only existed to me in textbooks and on TV shows, but now they were my everyday life—"My cubicle," I would jokingly say. They were magical, and I knew that I had a special place to clock in for work.

There is an undeniable magnetism about Southwest Florida that draws people to the region. Like much of Florida, the beaches are breathtaking and winters are filled with sunshine. But Southwest Florida has other unique draws. For one, it's a slower pace than neighboring regions. There's untouched land, wide open beaches, and so much wildlife. It's a nature lover's paradise. The fishing and birding are world-renowned. Miles of waterways are filled with fascinating sea creatures. Everyone cheers when they see a dolphin or a manatee, myself included, but truth be told, they really aren't hard to find. Incredible wildlife, unique plants, and gorgeous natural tropical landscapes; none of it is hard to find. It's a very unique corner of the world, and the people who visit Southwest Florida know exactly how special it is.

Over the years I had the opportunity to photograph thousands of people who were visiting the area. My clients were some of the most easy going, fun, happy people. People I generally loved working with. As much as I'd like to think that was because my charm attracted great people, the truth is, they were all on vacation and everyone is just happier on vacation. They were couples hosting destination weddings and families taking that special trip to Florida. It was a happy time for them and I was lucky enough to share in that joy regularly by being their photographer.

It's rare to meet a person who only visits Southwest Florida once. Many people return, year after year, for their annual vacation. Those same people would also hire me to photograph their families and friends every year too. I appreciated that tradition and I appreciated working with people who shared my love of the region. They didn't take anything about the gorgeous setting for granted. Most had been looking forward to this time for months, if not longer. Just being there and catching a sunset over the gulf was, to them, as special as the family pictures I would be capturing.

I appreciated those sunsets just as much. It wasn't unusual for my assistant, Maddie, and I to stay after our photo shoots, just to take in a little extra time on the beach, snap a few nature pictures, and watch as the vibrant sunset turned to night. There were very few days when I had any complaints about going to work, really. I did this routine almost daily for over 20 years, and I knew it was a unique gig. If asked, I would have insisted that I didn't take a moment of it for granted. Later, of course, I learned that there were so many things that I did. So many sights that I would never see again, so many things that used to be my daily routine. I realized later that I missed those mundane parts, epic sunsets and daily grind alike.

A drive, sights, conversations, acquaintances, calmness, and peace. I still find myself feeling nostalgic for things that I took for granted. Meeting Maddie and carpooling our way to different island beach locations. Maddie, by the way, is a spunky college student who shares my zest for life. That drive itself was always filled with laughs and funny stories, not the kind of moments you take pictures of, but still memories I hold tight. We would pass the same quaint little shops and restaurants and drive our way down tropical landscaped roads. Without fail, we would check the Yo! Taco chalkboard to see if "Krista" or "Maddie" were the first names displayed that day for a free taco, or slow down as we debated hopping in the dessert line at The Bubble Room, out on Captiva Island. We would listen for the music coming from the Beached Whale as we watched for pedestrians mindlessly wandering into the street. We would get pumped up for our next photo shoot listening to B103.9 FM, the local pop radio station, even though I'm pretty sure Maddie would have selected the country station if I let her. She would still sing along with me, only pausing to laugh at "misapplied-sunscreen-guy," or "too-long-at-the-beach-bar-lady" strolling down the sidewalk.

We would end up at our usual locales: The Sanibel Lighthouse, the historic Casa Ybel Resort, The Sundial Beach Resort, Castaway Beach Cottages, Outrigger Beach Resort, Colony Inn, Sanibel Moorings, the list goes on. I, once more, took for granted that just pulling into those parking lots was special, and something that could be gone in a day. Later, I learned that one by one, each of those locations where I so often photographed would be gone. Some closed for months to rebuild, some for years, and others would be completely washed away.

I miss those parking lots. No matter which parking lot it was, it always meant that I was walking into that gorgeous Southwest Florida setting that I love so much. A tiny winding path or a rustic wooden boardwalk would lead to a quiet beach, surrounded by sea grass and natural vegetation, large open beach areas, and the calm (sometimes almost nonexistent) surf that the Gulf of Mexico is known for. Granted, some area beaches had a party vibe, but most, especially where I found myself, were just peaceful and serene. Little hotels, inns, and cottages sat alongside the beach as more of a compliment than an obstruction. It wasn't like our neighbors to the east, across Alligator Alley, with high-rises and nightlife. No, it was delicate cottages that felt like you were stepping back in time and family-friendly condos that boasted their natural landscape; *that* is Southwest Florida.

There were always familiar faces we would see as we made our way to those beach photo shoots and weddings. From the friendly property manager at Sanibel Moorings, to the guy who pushed the ice cream cart on Fort Myers Beach. We would always chat with Jessica, JoAnne and José, the wedding staff at Casa Ybel Resort, and we would look forward to the perfect mashed potatoes they served at wedding receptions. There was Dr. Dan, the always smiling wedding officiant; Jana the workaholic florist; Steve, who always had his guitar in hand; and Alec, the wise beyond his years DJ. There was also a valet guy, a landscaping lady, and that one bartender at Outrigger too. Maddie and I would arrive early just to chat with those friends.

I don't know if I ever stopped and really appreciated those simple conversations. I don't think I ever even gave my compliments to the chef at Casa Ybel for the mashed potatoes we jokingly referred to as "life changing" either.

And then there were the obvious things I loved. The things that drew millions of tourists to the area every year: a coastline dotted by a chain of tropical islands, palm trees, dolphins, seashells and turquoise water. Those things all held a large chunk of real estate in my heart, rightfully so. I had conversations with tourists daily about what made Southwest Florida special. Many conversations centered around our quiet beaches and the natural setting, but those conversations would always inevitably come around to the locals.

If you grew up in Southwest Florida, you know hospitality is just part of the culture. However, a lot of the population is not originally from the area. So much so that, "Where are you from?" is the first question you tend to ask anyone you meet and vice versa. And I think it's that spirit of knowing what it's like to be new in town that makes it such a welcoming place. Neighbors helping neighbors and welcoming strangers into your home has been my experience living here. When you put it all together, all of the great things that make up this beautiful region, I think it's the most perfect place in the world. I know, it's Florida: the heat, the bugs, and yes, the traffic. But for me, those are all small sacrifices to live in an otherwise perfect place.

And it really was perfect, until it wasn't. In the fall of 2022 the strength of our community was put to the biggest test of all when Hurricane Ian set its sights on us.

I remember being on the phone with clients in the days leading up to the storm. Living in Florida, "There's a pending hurricane," is not unusual in conversation. There have been many times over the years where I was the calming force, assuring my clients not to worry. "The storm will likely fizzle out or not even make its way here," I would tell them. This storm was no different to me. I shared the familiar reassurances that their wedding day would likely go on as planned, that there was no need to worry.

It wasn't until about two days before the storm actually made landfall that I started to see that this one had potential to be something real. I had two weddings scheduled that week and just days before these clients were due to get married, their venues both canceled their weddings because of the pending weather. My conversations quickly shifted from reassurance to discussing why postponing by a week or two was the safest plan.

Many tears were shed in those conversations. All of the effort, down to the monogrammed napkins and party favors, with a now obsolete wedding date. My heart broke for each couple as they coped with the reality that on a day's notice there would be no wedding. Flights were canceled and travel plans were rearranged; it was so much work and so much heartache.

In those moments, as I listened to their pain, I couldn't imagine a worse thing to happen. In retrospect, that was the least devastating thing I encountered in those next few days. Weeks later, I'd find myself cursing under my breath as a best man gave a toast about the bride's "perseverance" in rescheduling and relocating her lavish wedding to a new (not destroyed) wedding venue on the other coast. I knew deep down it was still a hardship for couples, but my perspective had wildly shifted. In a matter of just a few days, I went from feeling their pain to being so angry about the mass devastation, the homes, businesses, livelihoods, and lives lost, that a postponed wedding no longer felt like a real problem. My empathy was occupied, pouring out for those that had barely escaped and lost everything. I listened to that best man's toast and I was overcome with resentment. How could someone be so callous and ignorant?

As I speak of the things I miss—a drive across an island, or a chance to get a free taco—I wonder if I too am callous? A loss is a loss and probably shouldn't be weighed, but grief is a creepy monster that doesn't always think rationally. I spent a lot of time in those coming months fighting that monster.

The day before the hurricane made landfall, its path changed. It wasn't until then that Southwest Florida looked like it may actually be the target. It had been predicted to go about 100 miles north until that point. It was time to take more precautions. My husband, Scott, and I filled the living room with our outdoor patio furniture, and we collected all of our potted plants. We picked up every lawn ornament, hanging plant, even the grill was rolled into the house.

Mandatory evacuations had been put into place for evacuation zone A the day before. Those low-lying areas are always the first to get notified to leave their homes and seek shelter. The sound of the emergency warning alert would come across my phone with each new update. You know that sound that is usually preceded by "THIS IS A TEST. THIS IS A TEST. HAD THIS BEEN A REAL EMERGENCY..." Only this was a real emergency, and that alarm wasn't a test. I don't remember how many times that jarring siren would take over my phone, each time becoming more and more concerning. Notifications for emergency information and shelters that were available flew into my text messages, then the evacuation of zone B.

"My home is less than a mile from zone B. Should we go too?" I wondered. Were we in danger? A mile isn't very far. I feared being stuck in traffic if we tried to make our way out at that late moment. What if we needed to survive a storm in our car on the highway? That seemed much more dangerous. Our neighbors were all staying. Actually, most people we knew, even in the evacuation areas, had made plans to stay.

I recall seeing a Facebook post by a friend the day before the storm. He asked, "Are my zone A and B friends staying or going?" Dozens of people, his friends, mostly strangers to me, all posted some version of "We are staying," in his comments. That post would later haunt me. I still wonder what happened to those people. I imagine many likely came to regret that decision.

We decided to stay like so many others. This was still a drill we had been through many times before, making that decision to stay or go. We knew waking up the next day to find out the hurricane had shifted directions was still a strong (and welcome) possibility. Unfortunately, that last minute shift that we had hoped for never came. When we woke up that following morning, we knew our fate was sealed. Hurricane Ian was coming directly towards us.

I would be lying if I told you I fully grasped what we were in for. There was no way I could have comprehended how this imminent storm would forever change my entire community, even if I had been able to see the future. Part of me is still wrapping my head around it today.

Ending Chapter one
What moments are you capturing?'

How many times have you said, "If only I had caught that moment on camera"?

It has become a daily routine that we take photos of uninteresting things. Our meals, prescription information, or a parking spot number; we are all inundated with mundane photographs. But how many photos do you have of you with each of your family members? With all of the special people in your life? Are you capturing the kind of moments that will be cherished?

More often than not, we find ourselves wishing after it's too late that we had captured those special moments, places, or people. If we had pulled out our phone for just one second, we would have been able to hold the memory close forever.

I wish I could say I had more photos of that gorgeous bridge to Sanibel; more photos of those friends who would move away quickly and indefinitely; and more photos of all those places that would be gone in the blink of an eye, but even I didn't capture all of those memories.

It's not just about the risk of photos being damaged or lost; sometimes, it's about the photos that were never taken in the first place.

So, I urge you to be confident pulling out your camera in front of others. Be bold enough to ask others to get in the photo with you, and stop leaving so many events thinking, "If only."

Just take the photo… Future you and future generations will appreciate it.

CHAPTER TWO

THE DAY

I t was 1997 when I moved to Florida. I had just graduated with my degree in photography from RIT in Rochester, New York and had vowed to escape the frigid Upstate winters. I bought a little red stick-shift Mazda, took a crash course on how to drive the thing before I packed what I could fit into that tiny two-door car, and hit the road, taking little more than my sense of adventure down I-95.

I hear people all of the time now say, "Those hurricanes... I could never live in Florida." But I'm not sure if it ever crossed my mind as I navigated myself down to the Sunshine State. All I knew was that winter weather advisories and wind chills were destined to be a thing of the past. So at barely 22 years old, with nothing more than a paper map and a dream to start my own photography business, I did one of the ballsiest things I've ever done in my life. I started a new chapter in Florida.

Within months I had a booming photography business. I was photographing families and weddings and even got contracts to do all of the photography for several prominent Southwest Florida hotels. My clunky film camera and I had photographed thousands of people in just my first couple of years. I was living my dream and loving being a sun-kissed Floridian.

Those first few years in Florida, hurricanes were the furthest thing from my mind. It wasn't a topic of conversation like it is now. Actually, I don't think I heard phrases like "hurricane preparedness", "shelter in place", or "hunker down", until several years in. In hindsight, my first apartment was undoubtedly located in zone A. Based on its location, that's common knowledge now, but that would have meant absolutely nothing to me back then.

My first hurricane memories were actually conversations about them with locals back in the late '90s. If you were new to Florida back then, like I was, you would have surely heard the local rhetoric as to why we weren't likely to be impacted by one. I would be told that for a hurricane to directly impact Southwest Florida it would have to enter the Gulf of Mexico, head north, but then put on the brakes and take a sharp right turn, which would be a rare occurrence. It all sounded very logical to me. I happily went about my business believing that and probably even perpetuating that fallacy until 2004, when Hurricane Charley miraculously made that exact turn of events. Devastating winds and consequent tornadoes left a path of destruction that is still talked about today. And proving that Charley wasn't just a fluke, was Hurricane Wilma a year later, wreaking even more havoc. And if still there was a lingering belief that we were immune to hurricanes, Irma in 2017 surely would have put an end to that. Hurricanes were very much here to stay.

Shortly before Ian's unwelcome arrival, local news stations were making hurricane comparisons, and I recall hearing that it was very possible Ian would have a greater impact than even our most tragic to date, Hurricane Charley. Charley had been devastating and trying to comprehend something worse was unfathomable. That storm had wind that snapped electric poles in half like twigs. My home was without power for weeks, and I knew several people who had suffered far worse consequences. It was a scary thought to imagine this could possibly be worse.

They predicted Ian could have the same wind but with a significant storm surge too. I wonder now, was I the only one ignorant to what exactly a storm surge entailed? Would it be a stream of seawater gently rising into a home? A high tide that could flood the nearest beach-front houses? That would be so unfortunate. I was concerned for my friends who lived near the water on Sanibel Island and Fort Myers Beach, but I nowhere near understood the amount of danger they were actually in. And I never even considered the danger that our inland communities could be in. A home that is a 45 minute drive to the nearest beach wasn't a place that even crossed my mind when I'd hear the words "storm surge." I wish what I thought I understood to be the danger we were in was accurate. I wish I didn't have to learn the truth.

By early morning on September 28th, 2022, there was no denying the fact that we were going to get the brunt of the storm. 150 mph sustained winds had already been recorded, and this beast was heading directly for us. The news had been showing images of mass destruction after Hurricane Ian had already pummeled through Cuba. Thousands of homes were destroyed, and the entire country was left without power for days.

Seeing the footage of what was left in its wake put a sinking feeling in the pit of my stomach. Destroyed property and people struggling created a gut-wrenching visual to watch on the TV. Under any circumstances, I would have felt that heavy sadness, that feeling when you start to analyze all of the possible ways you can help. "Can I send goods?" and, "Where do I make a donation?" raced through my mind. Rationally, I knew that was likely not possible. I've been to Cuba. I understand that putting together a care package and sending it off to a countryside community was not an option. I thought about doing a Facebook post, but it's not in my nature to be a social media warrior. You know—the people who share dramatic (often inaccurate) posts, demanding every colleague, grade-school friend, and neighbor four streets over, know about the cause. I decided not to be a keyboard vigilante this go, and to try and accept that my means of helping was limited.

I was sitting in a home filled to the brim with outdoor potted plants, patio furniture, and every random bird feeder and lawn ornament I ever bought. It was a visual that quickly brought my drifting thoughts back to Southwest Florida. All of that destruction was moments away from our own doorstep. I found myself rationalizing that reality in an attempt to ease my rapidly building anxiety. I decided it was a fact: we would have a different fate than Cuba. "Our infrastructure is so much better," and, "Our homes are built to a hurricane safety code," went through my head. I thought back to my time in Cuba. Power lines loosely strung from home to home, and leaning walls propped up by random objects deemed suitable by the homeowner was not an unusual sight. It was very sad, thinking back to the people I had met in Cuba and what they were likely going through that day. All the same, I convinced myself that the fate of Southwest Florida was not going to be nearly as tragic.

Dark clouds took over the skies that morning as Hurricane Ian began to show its ugly face. A heavy breeze and a drizzle of rain made for a harmless start, but it was a clear sign to hunker down.

The wind continued to grow stronger, becoming more impressive by the minute. Sounds of a sporadic breeze gradually transitioned into a constant howl. Heavy gusts began to make even the largest trees sway in the wind.

My two dogs, Van, an overly confident six pound Chihuahua, and Lyla, a Weimaraner with a more imposing size but much less secure in her fur, were glued to my side. Every move I would make they were never further than arm's length. I don't know if they sensed my anxiety or if there is some sixth sense that animals have regarding impending weather, but I believe both might be true.

Outside, every animal had disappeared, somehow knowing there was danger on the way. Birds, squirrels, butterflies and even an armadillo were all frequent visitors in my yard, but there wasn't a single creature out there. They too were hunkered down.

By late morning the power was flickering, but I still had hope that maybe those power lines would withstand the wind. A momentary power loss would be followed by relief when it would return. No lights, no refrigerator, no air conditioning would be an inconvenience, but watching the storm unfold on TV, that was a lifeline.

I was glued to The Weather Channel as they showed colorful graphics of the eye wall sliding into our coastline. I was hanging on every word, sinking further into sadness as they dramatically showed every map, graphic overview, storm chaser's perspective, and ground reports. I listened as if each reporter was sitting across my own kitchen table, speaking to just me. I'm not sure what I was hoping to learn, watching those same dozen images on loop while they emphatically shared with the nation the danger that was just outside my door. Its purpose may have been to provide information, but I was glued to the drama of it. It was a drama that I had invited into my house; I'd allowed it to sink in deep, and then didn't know how to ask it to leave. So instead, I poured it a cup of coffee and said, "Please, share more." I asked those weather reporters to unpack and stay for a bit. I started the day concerned, but that was quickly turning to complete despair as they began to show footage of places I knew so well being pummeled by wind and rising water.

The thing about The Weather Channel is that they don't show up when things are good. They are the one station you never want filming in your town, and you certainly don't want them to stay long. I watched that day, hoping they would be packing up and heading out quickly, but the fact remains—The Weather Channel would have reporters in our community for months. Fast forward a few days, and The Weather Channel was actually reporting right from my own living room. While I was glued to their reports that day, watching that roving reporter daringly fight to stand up in the fierce wind, I couldn't have imagined any of the things that were yet to come, including having him over to my house for an interview just days later.

There was some reassurance in the weather reporting that day, though. The eye of the storm, or the middle, had passed over us quickly, and that meant that it should be about halfway through, or so I thought anyway. A couple of hours and the sun would pop back out. That's the funny thing with storms here. They pass, and shortly after the sun shines again. I told myself that by 4 pm, we would be outside, cleaning up the mess, and checking in with the neighbors. I was pretty confident in my assessment.

But only for so long. I was hoping that the storm would start to die down soon, and we would begin to see relief, but as the back side of it crept over top of us, Ian became more vicious, and its winds, more fierce. I watched as the windows began to vibrate and bow from the pressure.

Around 12:30 pm, the flickering of the lights stopped, and the power finally gave out. There was no formal farewell to my coveted weather reporting station. The looping graphics, dramatic statements, and repeated weather advisories were gone. I turned to what I could get from the limited cell service and relied on what I could see out our own windows.

The high winds continued, raging more and more with each hour that passed. I think many things could have withstood the wind for a bit, but it was endless. Trees and small structures started to give up hope. There were constant sounds of things hitting the house: a tree limb here, random debris there. Each loud thud made me wonder if a wall was going to smash in and we would suddenly be exposed to the outside. I could barely see out the windows between the rainwater, dirt, and debris that had begun to collect on them. Scott and I would take turns trying to catch a glimpse of what we were hearing. I would maneuver my way through the patio furniture and past the dozens of potted plants that filled our house to peek out the dining room window; despite the mud and muck, what could be seen was grim.

The power of the wind was visible. Entire trees, strong enough to hold the weight of a grown man, were bending like blades of grass. I was too fearful to stand so close to the windows any longer. I'd peek for a moment, but quickly back away and retreat to the bedroom where I imagined I was somehow safer.

As I sat on my bed, curled up and hoping that the storm would soon pass, I was comforted by text messages from family, friends, and even clients from all over the country. They were seeing national news coverage that I was unable to see and their text message updates were like a gift from God. I am that person who keeps my phone on silent all the time, you'll never hear a ring or a chime while I'm with you. But that day, my ringer was on loud and clear, and those chimes were the most comforting noise I would hear. I listened for the messages and quickly thumbed out updates as if I were now the weather person reporting from my home on Hartland St. In retrospect, I was likely a bit too detailed and probably frantic, especially with people I don't know outside of their annual family vacation photo shoot but in that moment, all text etiquette was gone.

The fear caused by things hitting the house was quickly outdone by new sounds coming from our roof. It wasn't like the random tree branch that we had heard make itself known before. This sounded like construction workers in the midst of a renovation project on our roof. Bang, bang, bang. Then again, BANG, BANG, BANG. Was our roof blowing off? Were we soon going to see daylight coming in from above? The sounds continued. Scott and I had to almost shout to talk to each other over the constant noise. Scott looked out and saw it was, in fact, the roof shingles. He could see them blowing down the street. He called our neighbor, Phil, across the street and asked, "Is our roof still intact?" Phil could look out his window and see that we still had the roof boards. The sounds we were hearing were groups of shingles that were trying to hold on. As partially attached shingles would flap in the wind, we would hear the pounding. Bang, bang, bang.

A few moments later I called Phil back with a not very well-thought-out emergency plan. I shared that if our roof boards were to indeed start to fly away and we were exposed to the outside, we would be making a run for his house. I told him, "Keep the front door unlocked!"

I visualized the moment more like a scene from a movie. We would be running through pouring rain and a flooded street, dodging danger along the way. Luckily, that plan never had to be put into action. I learned the next day that a different neighbor had opened his front door during the storm, and the pressure blew out a window, sending glass everywhere. I think our plan to run to Phil's house could have had the same consequence.

If there was ever a moment in time that summarizes the difference between my husband and I, it would be what happened next. I sat curled up on the bed, giving my text message reports to anyone who would listen while comforting the dogs with some gentle conversation. I once read that dogs can understand as many as 80 words, but Van and Lyla surely know much more. They always listen intently when I chat with them, and I know it comforts them to hear my voice. So I was intent on doing my duty and keeping them distracted, or maybe I was distracting myself. Either way, I was keeping busy. Meanwhile, Scott was also busy. As I stayed firmly planted in bed, he was pacing the house making phone calls. I could hear him on the phone, "Yes, I need a tarp for my roof and a quote to have it replaced," he explained. At this moment the shingles were still banging and the wind was howling but he wasn't waiting for an invitation, he knew it needed to be fixed. I hadn't even processed what the next steps would be and he had already lined up the roofer. Then it was the tree removal service for the tree that had already fallen. "Perfect. We will see you tomorrow at 9 am," he said.

Scott is the most prepared person you will ever meet. While "let's wing it" is a philosophy I am perfectly fine living by, he has what I call, "A habit of doing things the right way." He is organized, he's neat, he never cuts corners. I hang pictures on the wall using thumb tacks and frequently forget to lock my car when it's in the driveway. No worries though, he always checks it when he walks by.

Scott and I complement each other, even in the midst of a storm. As I look back at those moments, especially of him being so proactive and organized, I think of how the next months must have been a challenge for him. Our entire world would be turned upside down, not only from the storm but as I worked to help hurricane victims. He supported me as I turned our home into a picture rehabilitation factory. He supported me as I continued to say, "Yes, I can help!" more times than I probably should have. He supported every twist and turn, and every random news crew in the living room too. Never once did he question my mission.

Scott continued lining up contractors to fix the damages while the pounding noise of the shingles echoed throughout the house. This continued on for an hour or so until they were mostly all gone. The wind continued as we waited and prayed that the roof boards on our 34-year-old house would hold out. It was already mid-afternoon. The storm was predicted to have passed by then but it just sat on top of us, seemingly standing still. 3 pm, 4 pm, 5 pm, the relentless beating continued on.

While Ian unexpectedly loitered in Southwest Florida, it beat down anything that dared to stand up to it. We watched as soaring trees broke in half like toothpicks in our backyard. An arbor, anchored in concrete with a 20ft tall Bougainvillea woven through it, swayed in the wind until it was finally picked up out of the ground and thrown back down. Slowly our wooded backyard became less and less tree covered. What once was an oasis was shredded.

My backyard truly was and is magical. It represents years of love and effort planting and trimming and building it to perfection. Dozens of old trees soar into the sky providing just the right amount of shade for the hammock that sits over top of a garden of bromeliads. One fence line is opaqued by a thick wall of fragrant jasmine, while another has dense palms that make it feel like you've walked into a tropical paradise. The patio itself is a swooping and winding group of pavers that circle around that giant purple Bougainvillea-covered arbor, leading to a quaint fire pit. Dozens of potted plants stretched from one side of our property to the other. They were filled with Bougainvillea that I grew from clippings, succulents and common houseplants that I turned into backyard beauties. I nurtured several tiny cactus clippings to become seven-foot-tall giants that filled concrete pots around the perimeter of the patio. Every glimpse out the window that day became more painful as little by little that was all destroyed.

Our neighbors' homes, that were never visible before, began to show themselves as the dense trees tumbled and limbs fell to the ground. By dusk there was a clear view of each of the homes that sit behind ours. Our once private backyard wasn't as private anymore and I was irrationally upset about it. I don't know if it was due to exhaustion or just misdirected anger, but I was not happy. My eyes welled up with tears as I looked out at big, old vines, yanked out of the ground along with the trees they were attached to. That day was the only time I cried over the destruction in our yard. The heaviness of the coming days and months would trump a damaged yard by miles.

That evening I continued to get text messages from friends from other areas with updates about what the news was reporting: "The Edison Hotel collapsed," I was told at 5 pm, "The Sanibel Island Lighthouse is gone," at 6 pm. My friend Greg is a producer at The Weather Channel in Atlanta, and I was hanging on every word he sent as if I was on a direct private line with the pope. The minute I lost TV coverage earlier in the day, he was the first person I reached out to. I had quickly become addicted to the updates and he was like my dealer, sending me little bits of my drug. I think in a rational state, I would have explained that Greg is an expert at all things TV production and one of the funniest people you'll ever meet, but he was in no way an expert on the weather, no matter where he worked. However, chaos, fear and confusion dictated the day. Greg was suddenly my hero. It was like he had some behind the scenes report that he could share before the general public would get it. He updated me throughout the day with what he knew; I imagine it was at the same time it was being broadcast to the world, but I definitely felt like I had some secret intel that I could place bets on. It's really amazing what you find comforting when you don't have control of a situation.

Eventually we lost phone service all together. By early evening I was no longer able to receive text messages and my last lifeline to the outside world was gone. The reassurance from Greg, the comfort of friends checking in, the updates on the destruction (both accurate and many not) had stopped. I would hit send over and over again, but very few messages would go through, and I assume there were many I never received either.

That evening there were only two messages that somehow made their way through the tattered cellular towers and to my phone. The first, a message from Gavin Newsom, the governor of California, asking for me to contribute to his reelection campaign. Now I don't live in Gavin's state of California and never have, so why he was texting me at that moment or why he even had my number will always be a mystery. I understand it was likely an auto message and my number was mistakenly added to a list, but the story tells better if we all imagine it was just Gavin, probably waiting for his Uber or in the line at the grocery store, just checking in to talk politics. He even included a nice photograph of himself, which really gave it a personal touch. While I would normally welcome an opportunity to debate the areas that I felt California could improve upon, I decided against it. Just to humor myself I did reply, explaining that I was in the middle of a weather crisis and asked if this was something that we could discuss another time. He, wildly enough, did receive the message and later replied, "Absolutely! Stay safe." I have since tried to get off of that text message list dozens of times, but Gavin and his team are persistent.

The second text message that I was able to receive was from a client. It was a very matter of fact message. She simply stated, "Now that Sanibel Island is destroyed we won't be able to go on our vacation, so we want our money back for our upcoming family photo shoot." At this point, the hurricane was still sitting over us, terrorizing Southwest Florida. It had become dark out and we could no longer see the damage but the howling winds continued. I later learned that at that very moment thousands of people were fighting for their lives, many had taken refuge on their rooftops to get out of the rising water. I could have replied with the face-in-palm emoji, but instead I waited a few days to send her a, "Thank you for your concern, we did survive," message instead.

I did refund her for the family photo shoot that could no longer happen. I refunded dozens of families over those coming weeks. Most waited to make sure I was alive before asking for a couple hundred bucks back. If anything, I would say most were excessively compassionate, a few even offering to just postpone their vacation and their photo shoot indefinitely. But there was always that one that didn't share that sense of compassion; the one that snuck in to my messages that night. While I sat terrified of what was happening, terrified of what the rest of the community would look like, she so graciously reminded me to also be terrified of what would lie ahead for my livelihood as well.

It wasn't until almost 10:30 pm before the wind finally died down enough that we were able to walk outside and see the aftermath. There was no light anywhere, no street lights, no porch lights, no lights in anyone's windows. Just an odd orange tint in the sky, and a breeze that was still moving things about. In typical Scott fashion he handed me a flashlight while he began to collect debris and sweep off the patio. I had hoped to get pictures of the thick mess that covered it in the daylight but he was on a mission. Thirty minutes or so later our patio was bare with the exception of the 20-foot-tall bougainvillea lying across it. Sadly, that didn't put a dent in the work that needed to be done in our yard though.

As we stood outside that evening we could hear a hum of generators begin to rumble. One by one, that sound would grow louder over the next hour or so as each neighbor started their respective machine. I didn't realize how much I appreciated silence until those coming days listening to that constant rattle. That sound could be heard from every room in our home. A non-stop hum that was a constant reminder that things were not normal. Scott fought with our own generator to get it powered up that evening to no success. I was so exhausted, I don't know as though I even cared.

While he tinkered with the generator, I investigated more of our yard and yelled to the neighbors within ear shot. "Everything okay over there?" A roll call went down the street with some version of "good here" from each person, confirming that they were okay. There was a power line down, crossing our flooded dead end street. It seemed there wasn't power to homes anywhere, and those lines were likely not live, but we stayed safely away, flashlights in hand, assessing what we could. Big, old trees laid in criss-crossed piles throughout our yard. Tattered shingles from our roof dotted what little was left of the grass, and random debris was everywhere. The storm was finally silenced, now it was just that constant hum of generators that filled the air. It was a mess, but we were okay.

I knew what we went through was very likely mild compared to so many others, though I had yet to completely grasp the extent of that. I later learned not to even speak of my experience of that day, of my own terror. It was insignificant and insensitive to even breathe the slightest word of it. I didn't know then that stories of actual terror would become daily discussions for me. Death, sadness, extreme loss, all would be woven into every conversation for months. Bearing witness to the pain of so many others would actually be the most difficult part of the hurricane for me, personally. Today, as I write this, I am more haunted by other peoples stories than I am by my own encounter with Ian.

I convinced Scott to give up on the generator that evening. We went back inside to the candlelight of our powerless home. I lay awake in bed wondering what the next day would bring. I'm not sure how much I actually did sleep that night. I can't imagine anyone slept well. I don't think there was a person in Southwest Florida that wasn't well aware that we had a difficult road ahead.

Ending Chapter Two
Are your photographs prepared to weather a storm?

There are easy steps you can take now to ensure your photos are protected before disaster strikes:

- Get a digital copy of all of your print photographs.
- There are easy methods for scanning photographs, including fast at-home scanners and even phone apps. You don't need to be tech-savvy to secure your pictures.
- Store those digital photographs in a secure online location like Dropbox, Amazon Photos or Google Photos.
- Create a secondary backup of those digital photographs on an external hard drive — Redundant Storage is always key!
- Make sure printed photos are in "archival quality" photo albums. This will ensure that the materials they are made from won't destroy your pictures over time. The photo sleeves will also protect your photographs from moisture.
- Always store albums in a temperature controlled space. Do not store them in an attic, garage, storage unit.
- Natural disasters are not the only cause of photo loss. Make sure to be proactive and back up your digital images too. In the coming chapters we will discuss these steps in more detail and give you the tools you need to ensure that lost photographs are not something you need to worry about.

CHAPTER THREE

AND THE AFTERMATH

My internal clock, the one that tells you it's time to get your butt out of bed, is set to about 8 am. One of my favorite perks of being a photographer is that I can get up anytime I feel like it. So alarms are rarely set in my house, and leisurely coffee on the patio is a regular morning thing. Sometimes that happens at 8:15 am, sometimes it's 9:15 am. And yes, I will admit the day after photographing a long wedding, it might even be 10:00 am. Let's just say the sun is up and warm by the time I join the daily grind.

I don't think I have woken up without an alarm at 5:30 am ready to start the day since I was a child on Christmas morning. Literally, I don't think the Easter Bunny even got that level of respect from me. I take my sleep seriously, and I have never been a morning person. There is only one exception I can recall, and that was that dreadful morning after Hurricane Ian hit Southwest Florida.

It was as if my body had somehow sensed that we were within moments of the first sign of light and knew it was go time. I skipped through a scattered version of my morning routine, brushed my teeth using a bottle of water, threw on an old pair of jeans, some beat up sneakers and a bleach stained sweatshirt, and immediately headed outside.

The sun still hadn't made its way up yet, but my neighbors had already started to gather in the street. I immediately headed out to join them, fully prepared to debrief. What had they been through? What did they know? Did they have information about other areas? I didn't have much information to offer the group, but I was pretty desperate for all and any answers.

They too were mostly in the dark. One neighbor, Chad, had found out that the printing company that he worked for was destroyed. The building flooded and ruined millions of dollars in equipment. Phil, who sold paper goods on Sanibel Island, and I discussed all of our mutual friends whom we knew didn't evacuate from the area. And Travis told us nobody had heard from his best friend, who lived on Ft Myers Beach, since mid-afternoon the day before. I could tell he was panicked as he paced the street trying to find a cell signal. It isn't unusual for my neighbors to all stand in the middle of our quiet dead end street and chit chat. I bought my house almost exactly 22 years earlier and most of the neighbors have lived there longer than I have. My daughter, Olivia, was just a baby then. She grew up surrounded by these people and they have grown to be more like 20 extra family members than neighbors. We vacation together, we do holidays together, I've photographed every one of their kids' weddings and we always rely on each other when there is a challenge. This day was a new kind of challenge though, one none of us were prepared for.

That circle that gathered in the street was ready to get down to business. There were discussions on who had what tools, who needed ice, and who needed gas. We discussed where would be the best place to start removing the debris and how to work around the power lines.

While everyone was strategizing on how to conquer the mess, I briefly drifted away as I had visions of acquiring a cup of coffee. I grabbed the coffee maker from the house and attempted to plug it into the outlet in my car, only to find out that you actually can't power a coffee maker with your car. I'm sure Scott would have rolled his eyes if he had noticed me attempting my mission. I had to accept that there wouldn't be the comfort of a morning cup of coffee that day. Instead of a warm beverage, my hands would get a pair of old gardening gloves. With that, I re-joined the neighbors for what would be days of monotonous labor, cleaning up what we could of our street and our yards.

We had just begun the cleanup work when a first responder that lives in my neighborhood came down our street. He was going house-to-house to check in on everyone. I saw him heading towards us wearing what looked like firefighter overalls with reflective strips and extra thick, red suspenders. He wore bright yellow rubber boots that splashed through the ankle deep water as he waded down the street.

He made his way to our group and asked, "Is everyone okay down here?" There was a nod from all of us as one neighbor told him that everyone was accounted for. The first responder told us most of our neighborhood was okay. He said one family had severe home damage, their roof was completely gone. He said many had lost shingles, that sheds and screen porches were mostly gone, but overall, we had fared much better than most.

That first responder was the first person who began to paint the picture of what had happened outside of our neighborhood. He told us he had spent the entire night doing search and rescue on Sanibel Island and Fort Myers Beach. He took a deep breath and shook his head as he exhaled, "It's bad out there, it's really bad.".

He talked about the flooding, the homes that were completely gone, washed away. People who tried to escape during the storm were left stranded, fighting for their lives, unsure if they would even survive to be rescued. He had spent all night rescuing survivors and helping them get to safety. "It'll take days to get everyone out of the wreckage," he said. "They are looking for more bodies too." I thought of all of the people that I knew that lived on those islands. All of the friends who Phil and I had been chatting about just moments earlier. What was their fate? Days would pass before I would know if my friends were safe.

The first responder also described bridges and roadways that were destroyed, and waterways that were too difficult to navigate. Island communities were completely cut off to the mainland. Getting boats to some areas was nearly impossible with all of the debris in the water. He said their rescue mission was the most difficult he had ever seen.

As he spoke, what looked like a military helicopter flew overhead.

It was followed by another, and then another. A constant stream of those helicopters would buzz by us. The rumbling sound of their propellers would become a constant noise over the coming weeks.

They were search and rescue helicopters. Those were just the first of hundreds of passes that would be made over my house. I never thought much of a helicopter before then, but they quickly became a sign of suffering. Every pass would remind me of how its occupants had likely lost everything. Those helicopters radiated with pain that I could feel all the way down on the ground. Thousands of people would be rescued. Thousands of people started the day before thinking that by 4 pm the sun would be out and life would be normal. But instead, in a matter of a few hours, they lost everything. Now, as they flew overhead, being taken to shelters, I could only imagine what they had been through. I could only imagine their story of survival... Or was it even survivors that were being transported?

Thousands of people would have done anything to have my hurricane experience. I learned that while I dealt with hours of uncompromising wind thrust at my home, thousands of others had that same force come at them in water. It was a storm surge. As much as 15 feet, gushing into homes with a force that moved things miles from where they once were.

As that first responder walked away, I stood in the middle of my street and just sobbed. The pain was unbearable as I thought about the people in my community. People I knew, dozens of them, close friends, acquaintances... What had they been through? Were they okay? The noise of panicked and unanswered questions filled my head. And what's worse, I was absolutely powerless; I couldn't fight back the tears.

My neighbor, Kaye, saw the tears streaming down my face and offered a hug. This particular neighbor is one of the strongest people I know. She is a seasoned business owner and a leader in the community. In the past I had seen her stand in front of hundreds of people to give a speech as confidently as she held dinner conversations. I had always admired her strong personality and confidence. Nothing phases Kaye, and I was so grateful for her strength right then. I needed that hug, and I felt her embrace to my core. She comforted me and said, "We will rebuild, it'll be okay." She then said, "You know we will come together, we will help each other, we will fix this as a community."

She was right. I knew we had a strong community that would come together, and I knew I needed to stop sulking and to think of how I too could be part of that mission.

This is the point where you might be thinking, "I know where this story goes... that's when you had the idea to help people with flood damaged photographs." As it turns out, you'd be wrong, at first I had other ideas.

That day, as I lugged every branch I was strong enough to pull to the curb, I thought through every possible way I could help: collecting supplies, serving food, cleanup, rebuilding—I probably made a mental list of 35 different scenarios, none of which were remotely close to helping people with flood damaged photographs.

I did have one lightbulb moment though. In the months leading up to the storm, I had been collecting some of my own personal nature photographs with hopes of creating an online storefront where I could sell them as art prints. It was a project that had been on my "business ideas" list for months. In the spirit of honesty, I will share that most things never make their way off of that particular list. It's not unusual for me to have 20 such projects sitting there at any given time. It was mostly photography related ideas, but it did include the greenhouse I was going to build, to sell the plants I propagated in my backyard, manufacturing my homemade dog treats, and the summer camp I wanted to host for families who couldn't afford summer child care. My already full plate rarely would allow for my hair-brained ideas to make their way off of that list, but this particular one was about to have a different tale to tell.

That vision that I had to sell my art prints online, that one was going to become a reality; it was the perfect way to raise money for hurricane relief. After all, they were nature scenes from Sanibel Island. My contact list was filled with clients from up north who all loved Sanibel, and they wanted to help. I knew I had the best audience for it. I would donate the profits to hurricane relief, and it would be a win-win. I was set on it; I knew I needed to do this project.

There were just a few obstacles: no internet, no power, and limited cell coverage.

There was no way I could even begin to build a website, and it could be weeks before that was even possible—but I knew someone who could. Over in Miami was the most brilliant young mind you'll ever find. A bright 22-year-old who shares my love for a crazy idea and half of my genes too. My daughter, Olivia.

I was sporadically able to reach her by phone and knew if I could communicate how to log into my Dropbox account, she would be able access the nature pictures. Then, she would just need to build an e-commerce website, connect it to the printing service, set up the credit card processor, post all about it on my social media, and send an email off to everyone on my contact list. Easy! Except she had never built a website before, certainly not a storefront. She had never set up a credit card processor, and she had not done a mass email either. Wildly enough, that didn't faze her. I don't know many people whom I can call with a project that includes websites, credit card processors, and mass emails that would even hear out my idea. I don't know of another soul who would stop everything to study 29 YouTube tutorial videos and some version of *E-Commerce For Dummies* to teach themselves how to make that all and more happen, but that's Olivia.

The storm wasn't even a full 24 hours behind us, and the wheels were already in motion. While managing a full college course load, her own social media management business, and her own list of volunteer work, she squeezed in building the most amazing website. Within days, it was live, and sales were already coming in.

My vision that otherwise would likely have never left the piece of paper it was scribbled on, combined with Olivia's fearlessness and tenacity, ended up raising almost $2,000 for hurricane relief. It was important to me to do something, to take action, to be a part of the solution. And I was, all thanks to my daughter; I found myself having one of the biggest "proud momma" moments. I know everyone thinks their kids are rockstars, that's our job, to be their cheerleader. I'm just saying, *Forbes*, if you're reading this, there's some serious "30 Under 30" potential here.

Outside of her work on the website, Olivia was also my rock during that time. We managed to get a few calls through that first day. A lot of our conversations were about the website, but she was also consoling me as I told her all that was happening. She's a great listener, and was a great comfort to me with her youthful wisdom, and it was definitely helpful to hear her voice.

That first day was a long one, it was like squeezing six months into 24 hours. We watched both the sunrise and the sunset while working, and yet it felt like we barely made a dent. It was a slow process, peeling away the blanket of crud that had suddenly filled our yard, and our lives. But little by little, we continued to collect the mess in a pile by the curb.

Scott and a team of neighbors were finally able to get life into our generator. The moment that ours joined the hum was the only thing I can recall us cheering about that day. The guys threw up a few high fives, and engaged in some vocal celebrating that could probably be heard several houses down. I did my usual Carlton-from-Fresh-Prince-meets-jazz-hands dance, and wiggled around our front porch as if we had just cured cancer. It was a small victory, but a victory to celebrate, nonetheless.

If there is something to cheer for, I'll be the first to applaud and if there is a reason to celebrate, I'll plan the party! We have half birthday parties in my house…Even for the dogs. Just earlier this week I had a bunch of friends over for a last minute cook out on a random Tuesday night just because I had deep cleaned the baseboards that day. But really, why do we wash the baseboards if we don't have people over to enjoy that with us?

Seeing as I had that group of neighbors gathered around the now functioning generator, I triumphantly announced my grand plan for us. It likely started with, "You guys!" because every one of my grand plan announcements starts with a, "You guys!" (so predictable). I said, "Let's plan a day next week, and we can all take our boats out around Sanibel Island."

My neighbor Dave, who has spent more hours on the water than your average boat captain, gave me a very kind, "We'll have to see." I wonder if Dave was actually thinking, "That's moronic"? He's the nicest person I know, and I imagine his thoughts are also pretty kind, but knowing what I know now, he could have said "Grab a clue, Krista," and I would have totally deserved it.

What I didn't realize then was that it would be a long time before our waterways could be safely navigated again. They were filled with debris, and when I say debris, I don't mean tree limbs and lawn chairs. Yes, there was plenty of that, but the real obstacles lurking just under the water were cars, sunken boats, even houses. Entire structures were submerged. Many waterways were simply not passable. And the water itself, with all of the contamination, became very unsafe to even be in.

Eventually, it did sink in that boating wasn't going to be a thing for a while. And even if I hadn't come to that realization on my own, the decision to stay off the water was made for us. The marina where we kept our boat had suffered severe damage. Massive docks had been washed away, some located miles from where they started, and the walls of the building were knocked down. The fork lifts used to put the boats in the water and half of the boats housed there were destroyed. The roads to get to the marina were actually destroyed too. It was almost eight months later when we could finally get to our boat. A few dings and scratches, but it miraculously survived. It was definitely nice when we found out it was one of the few things that actually wasn't "gone."

If I never hear the phrase, "It's gone," again in my life I'd be thrilled. That first responder was the first person to use the words, "It's gone." In the weeks and months following the storm, I heard that phrase more times than I could count. Landmarks, businesses, restaurants, parks– all "gone." "Did you hear about the Fort Myers Beach Pier? It's gone," became the starter of every conversation for months. With every loss I would feel a little more pain. It was the sadness I felt for people who lived and worked at those places. It was the sadness I felt knowing that some of my favorite places were just a memory. It was also a sadness for my own life as I knew it, including my business. As I learned of more things that were gone I was made brutally aware that everywhere I went, every beach I photographed on, every tropical wedding venue, they were all gone too. The storm had this ripple effect that started with one loss, but then spread to everyone. There wasn't a person in Southwest Florida that was immune to the impact.

The radio would also share the growing list of what was "gone." I turned to B103.9 FM, the station that used to pump us up before a photo shoot. Now, it was the place to hear constant community updates. I'd find myself listening to that radio station trying to learn what I could. Survivors shared stories. Community leaders shared relief efforts. It was a lifeline to our community in those first few days. It felt like an eternity before they would begin to play music again, but I was listening more intently than ever, hanging on to each word, trying to make sense of what was happening.

The sound of generators and helicopters flying over every few minutes was enough to keep the reality of the situation always at the forefront of my mind. Those sounds felt so tragic. Later, I'd speak to survivors who listened to the sounds of car alarms and security systems screeching for days as they waited to be rescued from the rubble that was once their homes.

In the coming days, my own family and friends spent hours navigating their way from Central Florida and Miami to get us more supplies and help with cleanup. For days after the storm, many roads were not passable and those that were had no street signals. The county has 447 signals, and 400 were broken. Stop signs were simply gone. Even I-75, our main highway, was impassable for days.

My brother-in-law, Chris, offered to bring additional supplies down from his home in Central Florida. What would have been a two-hour trip on a normal day, turned into a full day excursion as he zig-zagged across the state, attempting to bypass roads that weren't passable. Chris was turned back and redirected dozens of times before he finally made it to us with gas for the generator and some extra groceries. He even brought what might be the most thoughtful gift: Publix subs. If you are familiar with that Florida delicacy, you undoubtedly understand how appreciative we were for that special treat.

There were stories of people waiting in line for gas for hours, only to be turned away at the pump, and the few grocery stores that were open had bare shelves. We knew we wouldn't be able to get any supplies. Seeing Chris pull in our driveway that day was worthy of a celebration.

In those first days after the storm, we stayed close to home and out of the way of the first responders. The emergency workers had already arrived in full force. Police and fire trucks with insignia from all over, some places I'd never even heard of. National guard, FEMA, state agencies, they had all arrived.

The roofing company Scott had lined up had us on the queue to have a new roof installed. Over 50,000 buildings had damage, there was no time to sit and think on a decision. The roofer arrived with limited time and a full schedule to meet. If we wanted to get a roof within the next six months, we needed to pick a color immediately so he could order the shingles. Thinking on it for just a day could add months to our wait time.

Our house has been the same color for 20 years. Would we be repainting anytime soon? What color would we repaint? What color shingle would look best with the new paint color, I had yet to even consider. I felt pressured to quickly make a decision.

I later found that this one isolated situation helped me relate to dozens of people I would talk to who had faced that same pressure multiplied by many. People who had to rebuild after the storm had to make every decision quickly or face the consequences of not having a home to return to for even longer. What color floor tile? What cabinetry? What blinds? Every decision was an urgent one that they would literally have to live with.

In the end, I selected the same shingles we already had. I folded under pressure. I didn't have it in me to commit to any changes. I can't imagine how daunting it would have been to go through that for every aspect of rebuilding a home.

My experience in those first days is not a tragic tale of survival. I wasn't grieving the loss of a loved one or coping with a destroyed home, but just being in Southwest Florida was heavy then. We all took an emotional beating that was relentless. In some ways, it was more relentless than the winds of the storm. It took a toll on everyone and even my strongest friends would begin to feel the weight. I later witnessed my neighbor, Kaye, break down in tears. Like watching the last piece being pulled from a Jenga game, Kaye was that piece that was holding up so many others. When her strength began to waiver, it was confirmation that there wasn't a soul that was unaffected. It was too much pain for anyone to withstand, and its impact had gone far beyond the thousands of homes that were damaged.

Ending Chapter Three
Are your pictures secured from every disaster?

Being surrounded by people who were in so much pain and who had experienced so much loss eventually did lead me to helping people salvage their flood-damaged photographs. Through that I learned that for many, the loss of a photographic memory can be one of the most painful. Since then I have spoken with hundreds of other people who have also lost photographs, but many were due to other circumstances.

Situations that can cause damaged photographs:

- Water damage: Flooding, broken pipes, ceiling leaking.
- Humidity: Photos left in hot garages, basements, or attics
- Fire, heat and sun exposure
- Life accidents: Spilled wine, toddler with crayons
- Misplaced photos: Lost in moving, accidentally thrown out
- Fading and discoloration over time
- Mice, insects and other pests infesting or eating the photographs
- Digital images accidentally deleted, phone/computer stolen, lost or broken

Are your pictures safe?

Through my research, I've found that nearly 90% of people have experienced the loss of a photo. Statistically it seems almost inevitable, however, in the coming chapters I'll share some simple steps you can take to ensure that you are among the 10% that never experience that loss!

CHAPTER FOUR

LEAVING THE NEIGHBORHOOD

It's hard to comprehend what $100 billion dollars in damage looks like. I'm not really a numbers person, but I can't imagine many people have the numerical vision to picture that level of destruction. When I was graduating from college I remember having a final meeting with the bursar's office to discuss how I was going to pay back the $50,000 I had borrowed for tuition. I remember saying, "Throw in an extra $10k for yourself," as if I was Tony Soprano and I was going to slide over a few rolls of hundreds. The truth was, my $7 per hour campus job giving tours two days a week to prospective students was the only job I had at that moment, and that $50,000 might as well have been $500,000. It wasn't a number that I could even comprehend back in 1997.

I've since paid off that debt, but I was reminded of that moment when I first heard that Hurricane Ian had caused over $100 billion in damage. $100 billion; an incomprehensible number to me. Did you know that a million seconds is 12 days and a billion seconds is 32 years? I can't remember a fraction of the seconds in the past 32 years; I certainly can't wrap my mind around that times a hundred in dollars.

It was a few days after the storm when Scott and I finally ventured outside of our neighborhood and saw first hand what that level of damage actually looks like. We had finished the urgent work around our house. Without even a discussion, just a "What time will you be ready to go?" we prepared to go help others in the community. Our first stop was to help our neighbor, Kaye, to clean out her father's flood-damaged home.

There was nothing that could have prepared me for that first venture out. We passed street after street, lined with piles of flood-damaged belongings. Each pile was higher than my head, and stretched endlessly from one property to the next. I was mesmerized by all of the destruction, just sitting there, waiting to be taken away. Furniture and appliances were precariously stacked, layered with the unusual and familiar: crutches, a high chair, a framed diploma, a taxidermied deer head—there were miles of things in piles.

We continued on and saw homes that looked like doll houses, open to the world, with an entire wall completely gone. Trees were blown away; even a Banyan Tree, so large that it may have taken six people to put their arms around it, was torn out of the ground and tossed to the earth. And the boats. Boats in places where boats don't belong. From fishing boats to super yachts, we saw so many lying on land in all sorts of disarray. In total it's believed that over 7,000 boats were destroyed during the storm. The scene played on for miles.

As we pulled up to Kaye's father's home, we could see his belongings already lining the street. Kaye, who had been so stoic while I found myself in tears the morning after the storm, was no longer the fearless leader I had known. The days had taken a toll on her and I could see her strength weakening.

Her father's home, the house she grew up in, took six feet of the storm surge. Her 88-year-old father sat in a lawn chair in the driveway with a look of complete despair as he watched an entire lifetime of possessions being carried to the curb. I couldn't imagine what it would feel like to watch all of the things you once cherished now being handled as trash by family, friends and even strangers.

I put my gloves on and walked up to the mess that was spread throughout the garage. What were once stacks of organized boxes, neatly lining the walls, had since converged into flood-damaged chaos: Christmas decorations, books, tools, all spread haphazardly throughout the space. The first things I picked up were an empty basket that a gift had likely come in and a soggy throw rug. I carried both to the curb where I added to the growing pile of trash.

There was no conversation about whether something should stay or go, no, "Can it be saved?" or, "Does it have any value?" Everything was destroyed. Mold had already begun to set in, and the smell was unbearable. It was a pungent odor, one that lingered outside, but hit you like a ton of bricks the moment you entered the space.

A slick coating of sludge covered everything. The floors felt like walking on ice. The brown slime from the muddy, contaminated water had destroyed everything.

There was very little that could be saved from the situation. I looked around, and every item that I could see needed to be taken to the trash. Knicknacks, furnishings, and even memories of his late wife —all indiscriminately thrown in a heap at the curb.

The visual of Kaye's father, Ken, sitting next to his destroyed car in the driveway with his face in his hands, really hit me hard. A house he had lived in for 55 years, and all of its contents were destroyed. Everything washed away in a moment. You could feel the pain through the blank expression on his face. He's usually a chatty guy, but not then. That day he was silent.

I wondered, like the physical things that were lost that day, would Ken's independence be gone too? Where will he live? Will he move in with his children or go to a senior community? Will he ever get another car? At 88-years-old, would he spend the next year rebuilding his home of 55 years? I imagine that had to be weighing on him just as heavily as every other loss he had just experienced.

Ken wasn't alone. As I stood in his front yard, I could see people in every direction carrying their now valueless things to the curb. There wasn't a house in his neighborhood that had been spared; hundreds of homes, as far as the eye could see.

I wandered around to the back of Ken's house where there is a narrow canal. A dock, where I imagine he once enjoyed his morning coffee, was smashed into pieces. There was a boat lying on its side, trees crisscrossing through the water, and unidentifiable trash sprinkled throughout.

As I looked closer, I saw the most gut-wrenching and disturbing thing I had seen yet: The lifeless body of a black lab floated barely above the surface of the canal. It was evident that this wasn't a stray dog with an unfortunate fate. That dog had a collar on and a leash attached. How does a dog on a leash end up lifeless in a canal? Did its owners survive or did they share the same fate? Were they trying to escape when the water washed their dog away? Tragic stories of lost pets weren't unusual in the coming months. Many months later I'd still see "lost dog" posters with a photograph and a "Lost September 28th, 2022" written on them.

I quickly went back inside the house in hopes of getting that horrific scene out of my head. That is when Kaye offered up the welcome distraction of looking at the flood-damaged pictures she had collected. She had gathered pictures from throughout the house and had spread them out across the front yard: albums, pictures in frames, and loose prints too. There was a wedding photo, graduation pictures, a plastic cube that held as many pictures as it had sides. Some photographs were unrecognizable due to the sludge that covered them, while others were so waterlogged that they still dripped when held up. There were so many memories, now soggy, moldy and muddy.

Kaye asked me if any of them could be saved or if they all needed to go in the trash with everything else. In that moment, without words, I understood how valuable those photos were to her. Her childhood memories sat in that yard. The toaster that I had carried out to the curb earlier that day could be replaced. Those photographs could not.

I could tell she was overwhelmed. There was so much that she was urgently trying to do to help her father. She was competing with thousands of people for the attention of the insurance companies, FEMA, contractors, all while organizing the complete clean out of a home that had 55 years of life in it. We didn't need to have a discussion about the value of the photographs; I already knew. But I also understood how something so valuable just couldn't be a priority for her at that moment. Survival over sentiment. So, I reassured her—as I would later reassure so many others—don't worry about this one thing. I will take care of it.

I sat down in the grass and began to work on the photos. The bachelors degree I had gotten years earlier was in photography. A full four years of studying photography meant I left college with a lot of extra photo knowledge. Some would prove useless until that day. In the archives of my mind was a little nugget of know-how on what I could do to restore these photographs. I knew what the possibilities were of saving them and I knew what needed to be done. I also knew I needed to act fast. I sat in that yard for hours. I painstakingly cut every photograph out of each mud covered frame; I took each, one at a time, out of soggy albums. There were hundreds of pictures sitting there in the grass that day, and I cared for each one as if it were my own.

Most photographs are actually waterproof. The process of developing a photo takes it through a liquid chemical process, so they can get wet. However, salt water and mold are not forgiving to a photo. Days of soaking in that contaminated water and brushing up against debris meant that many were damaged. Acting fast to stop that degradation was important.

There must have been something intriguing about my sifting through these muddied photographs, as one by one people from the neighborhood stopped by to ask what I was doing. I explained that I was working to save Kaye's father's damaged pictures. I explained the same thing to each person that stopped by. I reassured them that water-damaged pictures can be saved, often by washing off that mud and salt water and digitizing them. I explained that even more severely damaged photographs can be fixed using some Photoshop skills. "Oh, really? Can I save my pictures?" one person said. I would hear similar inquiries several times that day.

These neighbors had endured deep traumas. They were coping with extreme loss, and in that moment, I realized I was able to give them something back. It was hope for that one thing; the one item that I would later hear over and over again, was their most valuable possession.

I left that evening with boxes of pictures to wash and digitize. We returned to our still powerless home. The hum of generators and rescue helicopters still filled the air, but now I had something to keep my mind off of those harsh realities.

I stayed up that evening, standing in my kitchen, as I worked on each photograph that I had collected. I couldn't stop thinking about the other people in that neighborhood and how helpful that little bit of information was to them. If the few I talked with didn't know the possibilities for their pictures, maybe most people were not aware that they could save them. I played through every way I could help more people in my head: knocking on doors, posting on social media. If I could help just one person it would be worth every effort. I went to Instagram and then Facebook, sharing my tips and offering my time to help anyone and everyone.

Time was something I knew I was going to have more of, and the reality of that was starting to settle in. There weren't going to be any destination weddings or families on vacation anytime soon. Every day I was reminded of this new reality, as I would learn of a new hotel or park venue that was indefinitely closed or even completely destroyed. My career, as I had known it, was headed for a long pause.

The job title "photographer" is pretty broad. There are a lot of things I can professionally shoot, so shifting gears was an option, but not one I was ready to consider. I was already doing what I loved leading up to September 28th. I was working in a place that I loved with people I really enjoyed. I never wanted to stop photographing weddings at Casa Ybel Resort or meeting a family at The Outrigger Beach Resort. So I dug my heels in, and committed to sulking over the loss of the work I loved. I was far from prepared to embrace change.

If you have ever read the book *Who Moved My Cheese?*, you may recognize my poor attitude as a character in the book. I know I was quite possibly living out that fable, but grief and depression ruled. I wasn't putting on my big girl pants—at least not yet.

The outpouring of kindness from friends, family and clients was a blessing, but so many included unsolicited ideas to help my unexpectedly halted business. I know that advice came from a place of kindness, but at that time it was just a bitter reminder of what I'd lost. There was no comfort in the prospect of photographing preschool pictures, car shows, and real estate; it was all salt in the wound. Every new "idea" I'd hear was a reminder that what I had was gone. I guess a photograph is a photograph to some people. Why would a dimly lit dance studio and haggling with parents to buy pictures not be something to consider? I'm sure my well-meaning friends were confused by my lack of interest. And truth be told, I didn't really want their pity. What I wanted was no longer a reality, it was gone. What I wanted was abruptly taken away and just like any other grief, there is no easy remedy that fixes that.

I look back at that evening, working on Kaye's father's pictures, and I wonder: was I consciously diving into these damaged photographs to avoid my own reality, or was it just a coincidence that it did just that? It was definitely helpful, well beyond the pictures. In many ways, it saved me at the same time. It gave me purpose when my own daily routine was gone. It gave me focus when my heart was hurting for so many people. It was filling a void at a time when I needed something to hold onto more than ever.

That night I could hardly keep my eyes open. I had turned our house into a makeshift photo restoration lab that came together like a field hospital during war: plastic storage bins for sinks, Q-tips, rubbing alcohol, paper towels, there was no time to worry if the process was archival or if it was up to the standards that I had learned many years earlier in college.

Each photograph was carefully washed. I lined every surface of my house with paper towels and would then place the pictures out to dry. My dogs would follow me from the kitchen to the dining room as I moved the pictures from station to station. I'm sure they were confused by my repetitive maneuvering, but I was happy to have their company as I worked well into the night.

I was pleasantly surprised to find that we owned yellow dish gloves, probably an item that had been under our sink for years with no actual purpose. Finally, those gloves had their moment to shine as they saved my hands from the inks and grime that began to run off the photographs. My hair was in a messy bun that poorly disguised that it hadn't been washed in days, and I was wearing a t-shirt that I pulled out of our Goodwill pile. At that point the laundry pile was already filled with the "painting" shirts and "gardening" pants.

That day ended like so many others during that time. Pure exhaustion. But this night was different; on this night I had hope. I went to sleep knowing that I had a purpose and I was going to fix something, even if just for a few people.

The next day, I headed back to that neighborhood where Kaye's father lived. I brought along Maddie, my photography assistant, and the two of us knocked on doors. I had already seen the hope I'd given to the people I spoke with the day before and I knew I needed to continue to spread that little bit of joy. So we went knocking.

The first place we stopped was at a home with a large picture frame that I could see heaped onto the pile of trash by the street. It was school pictures in a collage. We pulled into the driveway and an older gentleman came outside. I could see from his reaction to our offer to help that he was really touched. At first I wasn't sure how people would respond to a stranger asking to help in such a specific way, but his reaction just fueled what I knew we needed to be doing.

We continued on and knocked on doors. When we left that day we had filled my SUV with boxes upon boxes of pictures. We drove home with the windows down to combat the pungent smell of the moldy photographs. It seemed like a small price to pay to be offering people a real solution.

Another night was spent standing in my kitchen, washing moldy pictures, but now I had recruited Maddie for the cause. We took some bad selfies of the two of us and laughed as we stood there in our yellow dish gloves. Those moments were as valuable to me as the work we were doing. I needed them, I needed the relief that only a good laugh can provide. It wasn't our old routine that I had already been missing so much, but it was a new one. It was the one that was going to fill up days and nights for months to come. The one that would help dozens of people, save thousands of photographs, give me great new friends, and even have me on national news programs. It was nothing I had ever asked for and nothing I could have imagined, but it was exactly where I belonged, whether I realized it then or not.

Ending Chapter Four
Knowing what to do if your photographs get wet

Did you know?

- Most photographs are actually waterproof.
- If you have photographs that have been through a flood or even just had something spilled on them, rinsing the photo off in clean water is a good first step.
- Rubbing alcohol is also safe to use on most photographs. If there is something stuck to your photograph, a cotton ball dipped in rubbing alcohol can be used to gently try to remove the debris.

Tips for saving photographs in a flood

- Quickly take photographs out of albums or picture frames
- If photographs are in a stack immediately spread them out
- If photographs are stuck together, do not force them apart as this could cause additional damage to the photo
- To help ease the photographs apart or if there is debris stuck to the photo you can soak them in clean, room temperature, water for a few minutes
- Spread pictures out so they are not touching any other photographs. Air dry the pictures for several hours or overnight

CHAPTER FIVE

BACKSTAGE

Word had spread quickly. My social media posts were shared by people all over the community, and more and more flood victims were reaching out. Pictures were being picked up and dropped off constantly; it was a non-stop frenzy.

Within days every flat surface of my home was filled with photographs: some washing, some drying, some ready to be digitized and others ready to be retouched. Negatives were carefully rinsed off then clipped on a line to dry that I had tied from the oven door handle, across the kitchen, to a cabinet. That makeshift clothesline was a fixture in our kitchen for a few weeks as I cycled through packages of negatives. I was hoping that if I could save some of those, I would be able to replace photographs that were destroyed.

Many negatives were also in poor condition. The salt water had eaten away the emulsion, or the light sensitive coating that appears on the dull side of a negative. Some negatives looked like clear plastic strips with no image, even the orange tint was washed away.

Back in photography school, in the '90s, there was a required class called "M and P." I believe that stood for "Materials and Processes of Photography," although it was pretty widely acknowledged that it more appropriately stood for "misery and pain." There

I learned all the things that no creative person wants to know about photography: the chemistry that makes up film, the definition of words like *emulsion* and *silver halide crystals*. That class was an entire year and even contained a chemistry lab that I likely missed more often than not. I barely got by with some slightly embarrassing grades.

That professor was likely just as happy to see me move on from that class as I was. I recall his frustration with me as he would re-explain some complicated chemistry process as if I didn't understand how to sharpen a pencil. It seems to me teaching chemistry to artists is more of a punishment than a job. I imagine most people would choose serving time on Rikers Island with mobsters for cellmates over my teacher's fate. I'm not sure what he did to deserve that cruel punishment or why I had to be a part of it, but I'm sure he is just as thankful as I am that it's in the past now. Although, as I write this, I wonder if he will be surprised that I have a published book containing the words "silver halide crystals." I hadn't set out to further punish the man, but it is funny because I don't even recall what exactly silver halide crystals are.

As you may have assumed, I likely didn't take much knowledge away from that class. Not long ago, I would have bet serious money that nothing from it would ever prove to be useful. However, Hurricane Ian and some saltwater-damaged negatives later, next thing you know I was talking about emulsion in a photo lab again.

This time it was a local Fort Myers photo lab where I found myself using said photo lingo. I walked in with a huge stack of negatives. Most were scuffed and scratched, some missing entire sections of the emulsion with very little usable image left. I was hopeful though that there was enough there to make some new prints.

I don't recall the exact words that the lady behind the counter used when we looked at those damaged negatives together, but it was something to the extent of, "Hell no, we can't print from that mess." She called a technician to the front and then the owner of the shop too.

The four of us stood there looking at these barely usable negatives while I pleaded with them, "I realize that 75% of the negative is gone, but look! That spot in the middle, it's still there, crop into that!" My pleas, along with the word "please," (likely repeated a dozen times) convinced them to give it a try.

While not the most dignified method, I do know repeatedly saying "please," like a four-year-old trying to get a piece of candy, is actually an equally effective tactic as an adult. I once convinced an American Airlines desk agent to let me still check in for a flight that I apparently arrived too late to check in for. A full 32 "pleases" later, and I was on my flight to the Bahamas. I reserve this tactic for dire situations, just when the big guns need to come out. Getting prints from those negatives, even if it was a sliver of an image from the middle of a gummed up negative—that was worthy of some begging.

The reluctant tech took my pile of negatives and got to work. One family's vacation photographs, another on Christmas morning twenty some years ago; he was able to print from several of those negatives. They were pictures that their owners thought were gone forever. Surprising them with those now reprinted images was definitely on the list of wins.

Back at my house, the mess continued on with my kitchen being the hub of the operation. I always tried to leave a small space for Scott to eat his breakfast, but I can't guarantee that space was carved out every morning.

I had painted a picture of positivity and optimism with my social media posts, but Scott knew that wasn't always the reality. I was fighting back tears many days and saving these photographs was giving me purpose. He had every right to want his sense of normalcy back. For him, that was likely coming home to a house that didn't smell of moldy photographs where strangers' memories weren't strewn about, but he never complained. He knew this was healing for me and oh, did I need a lot of healing.

Part of the comfort of saving those photographs was in the time spent working on them. It was therapeutic to silently work alone, and when I had an extra set of hands helping me it was actually a little fun. Kind of like getting together to make a quilt or garden, a monotonous task done as a team isn't so monotonous.

Maddie was a regular, washing pictures along with me. Olivia would come home from college to help. My friends Jess, Cheryl and

Christine all popped in too. And then there was Kevin, a person that I wouldn't have even known if it weren't for the hurricane.

When I met Kevin, it was a couple weeks after the storm had passed. At that point, there were still obvious signs of the hurricane right outside my front door: a tarp covering our roof, the now open view through the neighborhood where trees used to stand, a small dent on the side of my car, and a six-foot-high pile of debris that lined the street and ran the entire length of our property.

The roof tarp was due to remain for a few more months; that now open backyard view, a few years; and the dent will likely drive around with me for as long as I own that car. But on that day, we were very fortunate to be seeing those piles of debris being removed. I watched out my dining room window as a team of workers made their way down the street collecting the mess. There was a giant double long dump truck with a mechanical arm that would pick up bits of each pile and place it in the truck bed. It felt like these trucks made up half the traffic on the road at this point, they were everywhere, and I was very happy to finally see one on our street.

The process was long. They spent hours working their way down the street to my house. When they got to my home I headed outside. I carried a plate of cookies that I had arranged neatly in an attempt to disguise the fact that they were actually from the Publix bakery. I introduced myself to each of the crew and handed them the cookies. They were very kind and super grateful for the afternoon snack. I think they were just as grateful to take a momentary break from the monotony of picking up debris too. In all actuality, I think they would have been just as happy with a sleeve of Oreos still in the package, so long as it gave them a chance to break up the day.

This crew had come to Florida from Louisiana and Alabama to work on a truck. One of the guys, Kevin, began to explain to me that this was a temporary job for him, as he was building his photography business. You can't say the word photography and have my ears not perk up. I immediately started asking Kevin 100 questions about his work, his cameras, his background and he was just as excited to share.

Kevin is an almost seven-foot-tall former college basketball star and recent college graduate. He definitely had a presence about him, but for as tall as he stands his smile is still what would catch your attention first. He is charming and sweet and kindhearted and as it turns out, a very skilled photographer!

Being a fellow photographer made Kevin an instant friend. I invited him over that evening for a cookout with our neighbors. We continued the photo conversation and I showed him the mess of photographs that covered my house. I was happy to mentor him with his new photography business while he shared ideas he had for getting a digital copy out of the damaged photographs.

It was interesting getting to know Kevin. I was fascinated to hear about the things he would see traveling throughout the county collecting debris. It was over 1,000 miles of roadways that were lined with the aftermath of the storm. It would be a full six months before a first pass was even complete.

Kevin didn't stick around that long though. Like many people who made their way to Southwest Florida to help, he realized that housing was in very short supply. I went on a mission to help Kevin try to find a place to stay, posting on social media and texting friends, but there just weren't places available. We found him a couch here or there, but, like hundreds of other workers in the area, he spent many nights in his car.

A lot of people I knew were already housing multiple people, both hurricane victims without homes and workers without lodging. A family down the street from me housed an entire water-damage-mitigation team in their garage. Cots were lined up in the garage for a dozen out-of-state workers who just needed a place to sleep for the few hours they weren't working. The family housed them for months.

In the couple months that Kevin spent working on that truck, he would stop by to keep me company as I tackled the photographs that filled my house. I continued to give him some business advice and career help even after he left Southwest Florida. I don't know if there are any other circumstances that would have put the two of us together; a young kid from Alabama and a mom in Florida. Olivia will tell you I'm quick to adopt extra kids though, and I've been a spare mom to many over the years. I am happy to have added Kevin to my roster of awesome young people to cheer on near and far.

My best friend Jess was another frequent visitor to my makeshift photo lab. She was more my cheerleader though. Jess and I go back to our college days in Upstate New York. She has seen me through some of my toughest times, from dating woes back in the day to helping me survive parenting a teenager; she is the friend that always has my back.

On the days when helping hurricane victims became heavy, when hearing stories of loss and despair began to eat away at me, Jess was the one to remind me of the bigger picture; how important it was to keep going. Jess has always been an inspiration to me. She has held a leading role at the American Heart Association, taught English to immigrant children, fostered hundreds of dogs, donated countless hours to charity and will drop everything to pick you up at the airport. She is a great friend and she shares my desire to make the world a better place. When other people were asking, "Why don't you charge everyone for this?" She understood that it meant more to me to help people than to profit off of others' loss.

Jess also did what any good friend would do, she distracted me from the sadness with a good amount of humor. She would find the odd picture amongst the piles in my kitchen to poke a little fun at: a baby screaming in the lap of an Easter Bunny that looked more like a character from a horror film, a cringe worthy 1980s double exposure portrait of a woman with an additional close up of her face weirdly floating off to the side, a lady on a motorcycle with a helmet that looked like something Snoopy had worn.

Jess once picked up an old black-and-white portrait and gave the most dramatic reading of the inscription on the back: "A union soldier in the civil war, honorably discharged at the end of the war. Grandpa George Bequest, born December 20th, 1844, died 1927. A dignified tall brown-eyed gentleman with a keen sense of humor." Grandpa George likely held that photo in his hands over a hundred years ago. Now it sat atop my kitchen counter as Jess and I made up stories about the life of Grandpa George and his keen sense of humor. Was he a practical joker, the guy who played pranks on his comrades during the war, or did he tell tales that would crack up his grandchildren? Jess and I would have the funniest discussions as we analyzed the personal photographs of strangers.

From vacation pictures to a creepy Easter Bunny, working on those photographs was like getting a backstage pass into a person's life. I'd see their newborn, their new car and their prom pictures all spread out across my home. When I was alone, I would pick up one photograph at a time to work on it and my mind would often wander. I was looking into the lives of strangers, peeking into the memories of the people I was helping. I was peeking into the lives of their ancestors too.

Similarly, being a photographer can often be like having a backstage pass into a person's life as well. There is something innately personal about photographing someone's memories for them. My subject has to be vulnerable and let me into their space for me to genuinely capture who they are. My career had always been focused on being the one behind the camera, capturing the essence of a person and that moment in time. This new path I'd found myself on didn't require a camera, but I was beginning to see it as equally personal.

Each person that I met to help with their photographs shared with me so much more than just their pictures. They shared their stories. Some told of survival, others spoke of the pain of loss, while for some the pain was simply accepting their new reality. There wasn't a single person who just handed me their pictures and left.

Maybe they felt that in order to fully explain the importance of the pictures, they needed to share more. Maybe they just wanted someone to listen and hear their strife. They were so desperately trying to save those images, but I knew they needed to unload at least a bit of their grief as well. I started to realize that also lending an ear and some hugs had value. I witnessed people break down in tears as they shared their sadness, each story just as gut wrenching as the last. People who I'd only just met were sharing details of trauma and then expressing their desperation to save what was left of their cherished memories. With each story I was reminded that what I was doing was urgent and necessary. It was my mission to give people, people who had been emotionally pulverized, a sliver of something good.

I was once asked by a reporter if this project had brought me a lot of joy. There was a part of me that instinctually wanted to say, "Of course, I've felt so much joy handing back restored photographs." And it definitely had moments of happiness, but it was generally pretty heavy. I hesitated to answer that question, which may have been all the answer they needed. I don't recall what words I did finally string together to express that it was a combination of both joy and sorrow. Would saying, "No, it's been the darkest time of my life," be appropriate?

Watching people desperately trying to explain their circumstances while looking at me, hopeful that I had some magic wand to bring all of their pictures back, was hard. The truth is a lot of images were just destroyed. Salt water and days of mold could probably take the paint off of a car; a lot of photographs just didn't make it. I wanted so badly to say to every person that I talked to, "Yes! That can be fixed!" But I had to share the bad news too. And it was heartbreaking.

Day after day, there were so many pictures that I had to watch people say goodbye to: the relative that is no longer with us, the childhood memory, the framed priceless moment in time, all gone. That's what hurt the most. As I hugged person after person, and tried to reassure them that it would be okay, I realized that those hugs were just as comforting and necessary to me—I was needing compassion as well. I too was grieving for my community, alongside each person I was helping. It wasn't my home, my car, or my photograph that was destroyed, but I still shared in their grief.

As the project continued to grow, I found additional comfort from kind hearted people all over the country who began to volunteer to help me. More and more people wove their way into my mission to save flood-damaged photographs. In every case, the kindness of new friends inspired me and kept me working, even on the hardest days.

Ending Chapter Five

Who is on your team?

With all photo organizing, I always suggest working with friends and family. For me, my team was Jess, Kevin, Maddie, Olivia, and several others that joined in the process. Photographs are meant to be shared and the process of digitizing negatives and prints is more enjoyable when you can share those memories in the process.

Do you have negatives that you aren't sure what to do with?

- Make sure they are stored in a dark, dry, climate-controlled environment. Avoid places like the garage or attic. Never expose them to humidity and avoid direct sunlight.
- Only handle negatives with lintless gloves or by only touching the edges.
- Negatives can and should be digitized. There are services that will digitize old negatives for you. You can also use an at home film scanner to quickly and easily get a digital scan.
- The life expectancy of a negative is around 50 years. Eventually the image will begin to fade or discolor. This will happen faster if they are not stored properly.
- Having a digital copy of the image is the best way to ensure a safe backup.

CHAPTER SIX

BUILDING MY ARMY

For months, there wasn't a day that went by that I wasn't working on a flood-damaged photograph. We spent Thanksgiving at my friend Jess's house because there wasn't a single empty table in our home. Christmas was the only exception. For a brief few days I slimmed down the operation so that our entire family could eat together. That didn't slow the work down though. Instead, those days were spent glued to my computer, trying to digitally retouch some of the most damaged photos.

I am skilled with Photoshop. The program was just a baby when I was studying photography in college. I took every course that was offered, although I'm pretty sure an iPhone today can do everything that Photoshop 2.0 did back in 1993. Since then I've taken more courses, gotten every update and continued to perfect my skills. Now, as I write this, version 25 is like working with a magic wand, which appropriately is a tool in the program.

Every picture that came into my home went through several stages. Before I began the Photoshop restoration aspect I would first get a digital copy of each one. I had set up a workstation in my dining room dedicated to getting camera scans.

My camera was on a tripod and I positioned old studio lights to bounce off of a large white poster board, evenly illuminating each photo. I worked with a piece of museum quality glass that I pulled out of an old picture frame to eliminate any glare. Each photo would carefully be placed under the glass to be photographed one at a time.

Like the yellow rubber gloves I sourced from the darkest corner under my sink, this setup was also more MacGyver than Ansel Adams. A combination of household items and dusty old equipment were enough to get the job done. Even the small table I was working on was actually our bar cart that was cleared of booze to make way for its new purpose. It wasn't the high-tech situation that I think people envisioned; it was the field hospital and I was making it work.

Next I would transfer those digital files to my computer, where I would begin to bring the pictures back to life. The damage ranged from a few discolored water spots that were easily removed, to entire parts of a photograph completely washed away. Challenges were many: a hand that needed to be recreated, balloons that needed to be put back into an image, each photograph offered its own set of hurdles. I would spend hours sitting criss-crossed in my desk chair, dogs by my side, cycling through pictures.

I would complete 25 pictures but then 100 more would be dropped off. The pictures were coming to me faster than I could possibly keep up with and I knew I needed help. Luckily, this was the one aspect of the work that could be done from anywhere. Anyone in the world with some Photoshop skills could do the digital restoration work. That's when I had the lightbulb moment of, "I need a team." I needed an army of volunteers to get through the work I already had, but I was already thinking so much bigger. With a group of volunteers I could help so many more people.

Where things went from there was all pretty much on brand for me. I have a habit of multiplying every situation by 100 and going a little overboard at times with my big ideas. Include me in your birthday planning and don't be surprised if you find hip hop dancers, an entire choir or a cigar roller at your house. I may even convince you we need to plan an elaborate group trip, have matching t-shirts, arrive by limo and be greeted with a signature cocktail served in a coconut with your custom birthday logo etched on the side. And I don't stop with birthdays. My attic is sectioned off by holiday. It's a sport for me to rummage through thrift store bins and after-holiday clearance sales, all to add to my ever-expanding collection. I've even been known to turn my garage into a photo studio for Halloween. I fill it with hay bales, cobwebs and fake smoke… You don't just get candy at my house, you get an entire photoshoot when you trick or treat here.

So in that same spirit of "go big or go home," I turned the photo restoration work into a nationwide project.

I started by going to the easiest place I knew of to find groups of like-minded people: the internet. I crafted a few social media posts explaining my grand plans. One post in a photographer's forum and another on my alumni page, both pleading with fellow professionals to help do digital restoration on hurricane-damaged photographs.

The response from volunteers was overwhelming. Dozens of people from all over the country offered to help. I created a list of volunteers and began to divvy up digital stacks of images. My grand idea to scale up the operation was working. The pictures kept coming and I was more thankful than ever to have gained an entire army of people to help.

Part of my daily routine was sending photographs off to these volunteers. I carefully organized thousands of digital images. I even surprised myself at how organized I was in keeping track of who had what digital picture. I had to create a system. It wasn't flawless, but it worked. That system had me chatting with my Photoshop volunteers daily and keeping up on a constant flow of work.

Through that process I began to get to know these strangers from across the country. In retrospect, it would only make sense that people who were so willing to help would also happen to be the most kind hearted souls, but it wasn't until I got to know them that I realized how special they really were. They came from all walks of life with a huge variety of photography interests, but all were putting in an enormous effort to ensure these photographs were restored to perfection. Their kind messages and eagerness to help were infectious, and a significant source of comfort to me.

There wasn't a single hurricane victim that had very high expectations for their damaged pictures. Nobody was particular about how a picture was restored. With a client, under normal circumstances, the shade of pink in the sky at sunset is something that might be discussed. With clients there are expectations of things being just so. This wasn't like that at all. People were so surprised that there was even hope for the pictures to begin with. Pictures that they thought were destroyed. Funny how things get put into perspective in even the most tragic of situations.

All the same, these wonderful, kindhearted volunteers still treated each photo as if they were being commissioned to restore the Mona Lisa. They each put time, effort and love into every picture they retouched. I would get constant updates on their work, progress reports, and even just check-ins to see how I was doing. I had gained several new friends in these digital restoration volunteers, and I definitely needed friends right then.

They really were extraordinary people. Nicole had the most advanced skills. She isn't a professional photographer who additionally has Photoshop skills, like I am. She literally works full time as a digital retouch artist. Photoshop is her expertise. She is the person that is on site, sitting at a computer working on photographs at catalog shoots. One day she couldn't talk because she was working on set at a Williams and Sonoma shoot. Yet, after her long days at a computer in her demanding career, she would still make time in the evening to fix a family's vacation photograph that they thought was lost forever. Every photograph she would do was a work of art. Those snapshots came back to me looking better than they did before the hurricane. To the people who had thought those pictures were gone forever, she had done magic.

The only thing I appreciated more than Nicole's skilled work was her kind messages and friendship. She was particularly understanding and aware of my circumstances. I knew she understood that this was a difficult time for me too.

I wasn't talking much to my new friends about the pain I was feeling. I was the "fearless leader" on the photo mission. I know, I doubt anyone was expecting a photo superhero, but I felt like I needed to be one. So, when I did talk to my new friends from across the country, I didn't mention my own pain in all this. The truth is, I was hurting. My drive to work had been reduced to rubble. That Yo Taco! with the free tacos and that live music coming from the Beached Whale, those places were empty lots now. And I wasn't even seeing those empty lots because there was nowhere for me to even commute to. I did my best to not think about that, so instead I poured myself into helping hurricane victims. But, that entailed hearing stories of families who were trapped for hours in flood water, fighting to survive. A family who had to break a window to get out of the rising water in their house. Another family who stood on their washing machine in waist deep water for hours, hoping it wouldn't rise any further and drown them; those stories were what consumed my mind.

I didn't have to share any of that with Nicole. She got it. She was sweet and knew exactly what to say, like a long-lost friend who reappeared at exactly the right time. I appreciated her messages. I appreciated that she understood that I wasn't a machine, only saving pictures. Rather, that I was just human and I was hurting. Her thoughtfulness, cheerful messages and even a card sent in the mail made her a shining light and her friendship a true gift.

There was also Greg, a retired photographer in Texas. He was also extremely skilled and happy to help. His skill level far exceeds mine and I'll admit, the pictures that I sent him were borderline impossible. They would always include a pleading message from me saying something to the effect of, "I know you will need to completely recreate half of this photo, but do you think you can work your magic?" It was always the most desperate of circumstances: the only photo of a family member, the special childhood memory. The thing with Greg was that he was always positive and always agreed to try his hardest. Those pictures I sent him were the stuff of Photoshop nightmares and would likely have made a lesser professional cry, but Greg managed to successfully fix every photograph I sent.

Getting pictures back from Greg always put a smile on my face. It was another victory, another time that I could tell a person, "We did it." But it wasn't just his extraordinary work that made those messages special. Greg is a faith-filled man and every message he shared included prayers, blessings and thoughtful words. One time he reached out just to say he shared the project with his church group and they were all praying for me in my mission to help others through this difficult time. I don't know if I had ever had a group of strangers specifically praying for ME before then. I definitely needed all the prayers I could get. My eyes welled up with tears as I replied to that message; I thanked him, but I can't imagine my words fully expressed the gratitude I felt in my heart right then. Greg was among a special group of people that gave me the strength to keep going.

And then there was Peggy. Oh boy, did Peggy ever drive me nuts. Peggy was an overly zealous volunteer, but I learned she truly has a heart of gold. Peggy is a 72-year-old retiree in Idaho who picked up Photoshop skills as a hobby. She was by far the most eager to help. Often that meant she was repeatedly messaging me to get more digital files sent over to her. Early on, when I was overwhelmed with soggy picture albums and heavy conversations, she wasn't my favorite person on the roster. Peggy would pop into my DM's like a bill collector with a debt to claim. She was persistent. She was on a mission to fix as many pictures as possible and she wasn't cutting me any slack, demanding I get her more files to work on as soon as possible.

In those days, if you saw me thumbing out a message it likely wasn't my mom or my husband or even my own daughter. No, it was Peggy. She also sought constant confirmation of her work as it was in progress. Was she restoring a shirt to the right shade of yellow? Can I confirm what was out the windows in the background of this photo? I recall one time, telling her that she could put the people in front of dinosaurs and they would likely be just as happy. Hell, I think some could have used that laugh. But Peggy didn't care that I was annoyed, she needed those pictures to be perfect.

I think as you watch from the outside, looking at a tragedy on the news, it's impossible to understand what it's like to live it. I knew Peggy meant well, constantly asking me to contact victims to discuss the color of a sweater and other trivial details. But at that time, I don't think a single person had the bandwidth to discuss much regarding their photographs. I was having a hard enough time getting a call back when pictures were complete; but I understood. People were over-whelmed. I was too. Shock, sadness, being pulled in a dozen directions dealing with damaged homes and loss of—everything… I knew that while this was very important it was also not a "now" problem. So, I did my best to remember the greater good of what Peggy was doing, and I would *try* to patiently answer her questions on behalf of each person. I would guess that shade of yellow and reaffirm that what she was doing was wonderful.

There wasn't another person who worked as hard as Peggy. She would spend hours at her computer everyday. With her self-trained skills, she could have been doing professional retouching, and I still believe she should. Instead, she chose not to use her talents professionally, but to instead volunteer to help people who had just had a really hard time.

As I got to know Peggy, I realized that this project was helping her just as much as it was helping the people she was restoring pictures for. I think she was just lonely sometimes, and she found a purpose in working on these images. Maybe when she was contacting me to get more work, it was really that she needed the friendship and connection those pictures gave her.

I learned that Peggy had once lived in San Diego and had a career that put her in one of the big high-rise buildings downtown. That is all in her past now. She retired and relocated to a small town in Idaho, closer to her children. Our conversations would make me think that she might have been a little down on her luck. It wasn't until a little over six months in that I realized how challenging her situation was. By this point, she had already donated hundreds of hours of time, fixed piles of digital images, and we had a pretty good system down. Peggy knew that I was going to jokingly tell her to just put people in front of dinosaurs, and I learned to just send her 50 pictures at a time. We actually became a pretty good team and I began to really appreciate her friendship. That is when she told me that she was going to be taking a break because her computer was broken. She was hopeful she would eventually be able to get a new one, but she just didn't have the money to put towards it right then. I learned that Peggy was on a very tight fixed income, and the computer was an extra expense she couldn't afford. Peggy had contributed hundreds of hours towards helping people, and I knew then that it was Peggy's turn to feel that same love. So, after pestering me for months, I began to pester Peggy. I told her I was positive that we could create a GoFundMe account and raise money to get her a new computer. She was surprised. At first, she said no, claiming that GoFundMe is only for people with real problems, dire situations. I explained to her that what she did helped a lot of people and I promised that now people would want to help her too.

Within just a few days, we were able to raise the money she needed to get the best new computer. I know the computer meant a lot to her, but I also know that the people behind that computer impacted her greatly. She was truly moved by the generosity, and I was too. I literally cried when I saw that we had met our goal. I cried simply because I knew how loved she would feel. After everything she had done and the hours and hours of selflessness she put in, she was finally going to feel that love in return.

It was people like Greg, Nicole, and Peggy, as well as the dozens of other volunteers across the county, that were truly bright shining lights in an otherwise dark time. Everything about this project seemingly just happened; there was never a grand plan. To say I'm surprised at how many friends I've made along the way is an understatement. The dozens of kind people, from so far away, have turned out to be some of the biggest blessings in my life. A surprise outcome from a time that I needed as many blessings as possible.

———————

Ending Chapter Six
Can the photo be saved?

Do you have photographs that are discolored or damaged? Are you wondering what can and what can't be saved? You may be surprised to find out that many damaged pictures <u>can be</u> restored.

- Discoloration and spots are often an easy repair.
- Restoration becomes more complicated when it includes parts of a facial feature, but not always impossible.
- Background items can usually be replaced. The experts I worked with recreated a Christmas tree, balloons from a birthday party, trees and many other items. Arms, legs and clothing can typically be recreated too. With new AI tools coming out everyday, those fixes require little to no skill and can even be done with simple phone apps.
- Photoshop has a newer feature called AI generative fill. It allows a user to easily add or extend missing elements to the background of a photo.
- With these tools available, it is becoming more affordable and easy to find a professional that can bring a photo back to life or to even do a simple DIY fix.
- A Photoshop expert can be found through a quick online search or on websites like Etsy and Upwork.
- There are also easy apps and websites that do color correcting, minor fixes, even colorizing of black-and-white images. I've had great results with the Photomyne app. There are also websites that offer image sharpening tools anyone can easily use. You don't need to be tech savvy or a retouching expert to give those a try.

CHAPTER SEVEN

CONNECTICUT

For several years, I have worked as a volunteer mentor for local high school students here in Southwest Florida. I hear many people talk about problems with the Florida public school system, and I know it has its flaws, but there are a few things that Florida does well. One of those is a program called "Take Stock in Children." This statewide program is designed to identify students who show promise and potential but who face challenges like financial need, and it offers them a college scholarship. The Foundation for Lee County Public Schools identifies these scholarship recipients early on, some still in 8th grade, and provides them with extra resources for success all throughout high school. Among the resources provided is a volunteer mentor. Of all of the various volunteer work I've done over the years, being a mentor is the one that has struck my heart the most.

Working with these promising young people is one of the most fulfilling things I've ever done. In 2023, I was actually named "Mentor of the Year," which, to me, is about the biggest honor there is. I accepted that plaque as if I had gotten the Nobel Peace Prize. I definitely took a solid 30 selfies with it and immediately called my mom.

What, with my love of working with students and my innate need to turn everything into a bit of a production, it would only be natural that I rallied a group of students to join my cause. But, I'm embarrassed to say, I didn't think of that. Fortunately, I do believe that a greater power had my back and knew exactly where this project needed to go. That's when Miss Toto appeared in my inbox.

Miss Toto is a teacher at Amity High School in Connecticut. She had seen an interview I had done with *ABC World News Tonight* with David Muir and immediately reached out. Her message read, "I'm contacting you because my Digital Photo students are restoring damaged photos." She continued, "My students really want to get involved in your project…real people's loss. A great lesson in skill and empathy. And, by the way, my students are good at it." She had the highest confidence in her students, offering that they start working to help restore photographs right away.

I absolutely loved the idea. The digital restoration work itself covered a huge range of skill levels. Some images just needed to be cropped in closer to eliminate damaged edges, while others needed much more attention. That made these images great work for students because it gave them the chance to use a range of different Photoshop functions.

I immediately organized the first group of digital photographs and sent them off to her. Within days they had completed the work and were ready for more pictures. Some of the most impressive restoration work I had seen came from those young students. Early on, Miss Toto had made it a class assignment to work on the pictures, but then after a few weeks she returned to her regular curriculum. However, the students continued to work on the hurricane-damaged photographs, now for extra credit. Every single student in the class continued to stay after school, came in during study hall, and even during lunch to keep the project going.

Throughout that entire semester, I had daily conversations with Miss Toto. What started as factual accounts of progress on the photographs quickly turned to conversations about her classroom, her feelings on teaching, and her struggles. She is the type of person that puts 200% into everything she does, and I could definitely relate to that. I thought many times how fortunate her students are to have her as their teacher. She is truly a gem, and the world is a better place with her in it.

At the end of the semester, the students had completed hundreds of photographs. It was the single largest group of restored pictures in the project. Miss Toto wanted to honor the students for their hard work and organized a gathering where the students could meet some of the people they had helped via zoom. She also wanted me to join via zoom and meet these amazing young people too. I gave it a little thought and suggested I do one better: why don't I fly up there and meet everyone in person?! She was thrilled at the idea. She reminded me that January in Connecticut might be a shock to my Florida system, but I was prepared to brave the cold for the opportunity to meet her and her class in person.

I pulled out a box of winter clothing that I keep tucked in the far back corner of my closet. I packed the scarf, mittens and oversized coat that rarely see the light of day, and convinced Olivia to join me on a winter adventure. With just a couple weeks notice, we headed north.

We got flights to New York City. From there we took a two-hour train ride, followed by an Uber, to finally arrive at Amity High School. We quickly scurried out of the cold into the welcoming little school. There, we were immediately greeted by Miss Toto and a group of very proud students.

They showed me their work stations and the skills Miss Toto had taught them. They shared some very impressive work that they had done restoring hurricane-damaged photographs. A family heirloom picture from the 1800s was skillfully given a facelift. A school photo from the '50s looked brand new. There were dozens of restored photographs printed and spread throughout the room. I could have spent hours looking at those pictures and discussing the students' hard work, but we quickly moved on to the other activities of that day.

A local Connecticut news crew was there to interview the students, and *ABC World News Tonight* sent a camera person to do a follow up on the story they had done with me as well. Those interviews continued throughout the morning as people filed in and out of the room to see what all of the hubbub was about. The principal came by to say hello, and then the school superintendent arrived as well.

The room had the energy of a wedding reception. There was a kind of positive chaos that made time fly by at record speed. Olivia and I were introduced to dozens of people, names I've mostly forgotten, but everyone was so excited to see the work the students had done and to hear more about the project.

I was able to arrange zoom meetings with two of the people the students had helped. A large screen and projector were set up so the entire room could be a part of each meeting. As the zoom began, each student walked up to the camera, one at a time, and held up a large print of a photograph they had restored. There were several moments that the entire room (and zoom) was brought to tears. One woman saw a restored photo of her late mother holding her baby son (now 40 years old). She wept as she looked at the photo being held up to the computer camera.

One of the zoom meetings was with my neighbor Kaye. I had gone back to Kaye's father's house a few days after she had lined the yard with photographs. I was in the neighborhood to see if there was anyone else I could help and thought I'd stop by and see how the progress was coming along at her father's home. Kaye wasn't there, she had to return to work, but her brother, Gerry, had driven over from the other coast of Florida to continue the clean up efforts. When I arrived Gerry had found more photographs that needed help. These weren't like the frames and albums that Kaye had brought out, these were boxes of loose pictures. Hidden treasures of sorts. Things that even Kaye's father forgot he owned.

As I was sorting through the new piles of photographs I found some really special moments: Kaye as a child, with her late mother, pictures of her parents together and fun moments from their family travels. Those were among the many pictures that I had sent off to Miss Toto's class.

It was always a special moment, seeing a family react to photographs that they thought they lost, but it was different watching Kaye see pictures for what may have been the first time ever. Those photographs that had been hidden away were found, and now she was seeing these special images for the first time. She eloquently explained to the students how much this meant to her, how they had saved a part of her family history.

When the students began this work they didn't know the stories behind the photos or the people each belonged to, they just knew that it was a way to fix a small part of a big problem. The people they helped were complete strangers to them, but now, for the first time, they were no longer just faces in a photograph. I looked around the room at the students. Each was glued to the projection screen, many had tears in their eyes. I could tell this meant something to them; restoring these photographs would forever impact a lot more people than I could have ever initially imagined.

The festivities concluded with the most heartfelt presentation down the hall in the school library. More students and teachers joined us. It was standing room only as people were eager to see what the students had accomplished. Miss Toto spoke about the impact her students had made and how they had shown enormous amounts of empathy and compassion. Then I was invited to the front of the room to address the group.

I don't recall my exact words, but I doubt they adequately expressed how proud I was of them at that moment. Their dedication and selflessness had really impressed me. I know I thanked them for their hard work, and I made sure that everyone in the room knew the impact that they had. I congratulated them on a successful semester and dished out some of my signature encouragement. I only hope that each student could feel my pride, even if my words didn't do it justice. I hope that their work on these photographs leaves a mark on their hearts that will stay with them forever.

At the conclusion of the presentation, the students were all dismissed, but several stayed behind to talk more. As I stood in the front of the room, a group of them made their way towards me, hoping to ask more questions. They asked specifics about the project, about being a professional photographer, about Southwest Florida, and Hurricane Ian. I was already fully convinced that they were truly invested in this work, but seeing them want to continue the conversation was really sweet.

I imagine it's a challenge for a teacher to find a way to keep students interested, but Miss Toto did just that. She knew when she saw the story on the news that this was exactly what her students needed, and she was so right.

Miss Toto let the students talk for a bit before she reminded them they needed to move on to their last class of the day. An impromptu hug line formed, and I gave each student a quick embrace before they turned to run out the door. I don't think I could fit any more joy in me than what I felt in that moment. That conversation and those kind hugs were everything; they sent that spectacular day out with a bang.

We only spent that one afternoon with the students. Olivia and I were back to the train station by evening. I had a lot to digest on the long ride back. I don't think Olivia and I spoke a word; I just sat there, quietly thinking about the whirlwind of a day we just had. I thought about all of the negative generalizations that are made about kids today and how this class disproved anything bad I'd ever heard. It wasn't just one kid; it was the entire group, all radiating positivity and huge, caring hearts. It was definitely more fuel for me to continue on with the mission.

When I returned, I continued to keep in touch with Miss Toto and her class. I even did a FaceTime call with them at the opening night of their photography gallery show that spring. Those students worked tirelessly on hurricane-damaged photographs all year, but then also kept up on their other photography work too. They put on the most professional presentation of photographs they had taken throughout the year, and I was happy to have a virtual invitation to be able to see their work and to see them again.

A few months after my visit to the school, a woman that the students had helped with damaged photographs reached out to me. She suggested that we put a plaque together to honor the students for their hard work. "Brilliant," I thought. She offered to create it and send it to the students. I was in tears when I got to see it complete. It said: "From the Southwest Florida Families impacted by Hurricane Ian, we are forever grateful for your talent, skill and generosity in the restoration of our most cherished memories. Thank you."

This work had a completely unpredictable way of weaving its way into hearts, and the goodness that would come from it continually went beyond just pictures. From the generosity of the students to the thoughtfulness of the family who created the plaque, there was so much goodness coming from people.

I imagine that plaque will remain at the school. I envision it proudly displayed as a reminder for the students, they made a difference in the lives of people 1,300 miles away. Future classes at Amity High School will hopefully take notice and talk about that year when Miss Toto's class cared a little extra and went above and beyond for complete strangers.

Ending Chapter Seven
Start by getting a digital copy of every photograph

Before I would send photographs off to Miss Toto, I would make sure to get a quality scan of each picture. Back then, I used my professional 35mm camera to create digital copies. However, I've since discovered easier methods that anyone can use with great results—no professional equipment required.

One of the simplest ways to digitize photos is by using a phone app. Apps like Photomyne or Google Photoscan (which is free) are excellent options for creating digital copies directly from your phone. If you're looking for the best possible results, consider investing in an at-home scanner like The Epson FastFoto, which is specifically designed for preserving photos.

Over the years, I've taught hundreds of people how to digitize and secure their own pictures using these methods. Once you have digital copies, you'll have the freedom to organize, edit, and preserve them, ensuring your memories are safe for generations to come.

Tips for scanning photographs

First, remove all of the photographs from photo albums. They will scan better if they are not in plastic pages. Put pictures in chronological order before scanning.

Scanning photographs using an app

- Download a photo scanning app to your phone.
- Find an area that has bright natural light - Avoid direct sunlight, dark rooms and overhead lights or lamps.
- Each app has easy instructions that will guide you through capturing a scan.
- If you are seeing a glare in your scans a piece of museum quality glass from any framer placed over the photo will help to eliminate some glare and help to keep a photo flat.
- I've worked with children as young as 6 years old who have successfully helped me digitize old photographs using an app. This project is a fun family activity. Be sure to take your time, discuss the photographs and enjoy the process!

How to get a digital scan of a photograph using a home scanner

- Choose a scanner. Flatbed scanners tend to be the most affordable option, however, they are the most time consuming method. I suggest a scanner with a photo feeder. Although more expensive, this is the fastest scanning method.
- This method requires a computer and downloading software. The process is typically simple and easy to accomplish.
- Then follow your scanners simple instructions to begin to get those digital scans.
- Remember! Organizing pictures isn't like cleaning the garage. It's personal and often emotional. Take time to reflect on the memories and enjoy the treasures that you find.

CHAPTER EIGHT

CAPE CORAL

You had to have known, at some point in this book, I was going to ask—Where are your own photographs stored? Are your old prints digitized? Are the pictures on your phone backed up? Are they printed? If I could give this book one overall goal it's that you leave here motivated to tackle these questions with tangible solutions. You see, everyone, and I mean every single person I've helped, could have avoided a lot of grief had they done a little preparation. None of them thought it would happen to them. Each painful story is drenched in regret, and I know today that each person would share my plea with you too: Now is the time to be proactive and to secure your own photographs.

One of those victims whom I know would share that sentiment, is Lori.

In the first weeks after the hurricane, I was completely immersed in pictures, so much so that my house was full and my time was all but consumed. I had gotten to a point that I needed to be a little less zealous in agreeing to take on every photograph that came my way. I didn't want to accept anything that I wasn't positive I could successfully restore.

That's when I was tagged in a post in a forum on Facebook. It was

Lori's adult son, Jeffery. Jeffery posted that his parents' home was flooded, and they didn't know what to do about their pictures. Someone familiar with my work suggested that he talk to me. We spoke on the phone, and he explained that his mom, Lori, had thousands of flood-damaged pictures she didn't know what to do with.

I could feel the sadness in his voice as he shared their story. It was another heartbreaking situation that ended with everything they owned heaped at the curb. It was a story I had heard so many times, a story that had become way too familiar.

The day before the storm, Lori was reluctant to leave their home and didn't evacuate until the last minute. Luckily, they did manage to get to higher ground, and it proved to be a very wise decision. But unfortunately, all of their family photographs were among the items that were left behind.

I connected with Lori's husband, David, and set up a time when we could meet at their flood-damaged home to look at the pictures. My intention was to look at what they had collected, give them advice on what they could do themselves, and take with me a small group of photos that I would be able to work on more.

A few things struck me about this particular family. As I arranged to meet them, I learned that Lori wouldn't be able to meet me in person because she had to be at work. She had to go back to work as soon as the storm had passed. I know that in a way, it seems obvious that the world keeps moving and life goes on, work included. But it baffled me that half of the community was dealing with home damage, and yet it was still to some effect "business as usual." So Lori's home was destroyed, and then she went to work while other people came in and cleaned out her house. I can't imagine losing your possessions and not even being the one to see them off. I hadn't even met Lori yet, but my heart already hurt for her.

Another interesting thing about Lori's family was that their home was a duplex, split into two homes. One half was where her elderly mother and step-father resided, and Lori and David lived on the other side; so their photograph collection spanned many generations. They had photographs going as far back as the late 1800s, and all of them had been water damaged.

As I made my way to Lori's house, I passed more destruction. Her home is in Cape Coral, sitting 16 miles away from Kaye's father's home in North Fort Myers. It is 20 miles the other direction to Sanibel Island, where there were others I would help. The sheer span of the flooding was huge. In total, Ian stretched more than 140 miles, which is longer than the length of the Jersey Shore, or the entire coastline of Georgia or Virginia. It far surpassed the size of Hurricane Charley. That powerful hurricane was comparatively a tiny baby that could have fit entirely inside the eye of Hurricane Ian.

Floridians all know about hurricane damage from wind. Wind is selective though. It will impact one house and not the next. Ian had those high winds, but it was the flooding that refused to spare anything in its path. And that path wasn't through a single neighborhood or even town; it was mile after mile, community after community, with no break in the destruction.

Many of the people I helped lived nowhere near each other. Their kids wouldn't have gone to school together, they would have gone to different churches, and they likely never bumped into each other at the grocery store. Actually, some lived twelve Publix supermarkets away from each other. Yet they all had their lives turned upside down on that same single day. Each with the same story of muddy water ravaging their homes. Water that came in with force, and busted through everywhere and everything like a freight train.

I tried not to gawk as I made my way through Lori's neighborhood, but some things were just too shocking to look away from: a boat blocking a lane on the street, a tree being supported by a car, unimaginable scenes around every corner. Miles of roadways piled high with things that in a matter of a day had gone from valuables to trash.

When I arrived, Lori's husband, David greeted me. I could see the damage right away. Their home was not livable, and most everything was destroyed. The place had been in their family since the 1960s and had stood up to many storms over the years. It met its match in Hurricane Ian.

As I stood on what was left of their property, I thought hard about the house I live in. When I purchased my home many years ago, there were visions of all of the things that would come, the memories that would be built in that space. So many of the things I imagined did happen within those walls: Olivia's first day of kindergarten, her high school graduation party, sleepovers, dinner parties, holiday celebrations, welcoming new pets. There were all of the times I pulled out my camera, just to make sure a moment was captured. But there were also the ones that weren't: all of the baking fails, the impromptu dance parties, the movie nights. Those memories are simply held in the walls themselves.

I looked at the remnants of the walls in David and Lori's home and I knew they too once held their own stories. Now they just held an eerie feeling that filled the space; a cold, chilling air, much like a haunted house. Only it wasn't ghosts that lingered, it was sadness and despair.

David led me around to the back of their home where they had a tall Rubbermaid storage shed. He pulled open the double doors to reveal neatly organized stacks of rubber totes. This space had clearly been designated to store the items they had hoped to save. There wasn't much, and what was there probably wouldn't even fill the bed of a small pick up truck, but it was everything they had left.

Piled in with those rubber totes were also six black trash bags completely filled with photo albums. We pulled the heavy bags to the ground, where I opened each to review its contents. I was immediately hit by the pungent smell of mold as we opened those sealed bags. There were dozens of photo albums, all still dripping water.

I gave David the game plan for what needed to happen with the albums. "A digital scan should be made of each picture, there are easy apps you can install on your phone to help you do that," I explained. "Every photo needs to be cut out of the album first though, rinsed off and set out to dry."

As I was saying this, I knew that he already had his hands full. Work crews were scurrying around the property, and the business of their rebuild had already begun. Tools and building supplies were strewn about their yard. They hadn't even gotten power or running water back, but they weren't waiting. They were determined to be back in that home as soon as possible. Inevitably, the photographs quickly moved down the to-do list.

I knew they likely didn't have the time or space to work on the pictures themselves, but I asked David anyway, "Which of these are the most important?" We stood there together, staring at the now half open trash bags spread across the yard. I told him I could take a small group that day to start working on, but deep down I already knew where this was going. "A small group" was likely going to be all of them and I already knew that. I don't know if David could see my mind turning. It was somewhere between, "I'll add folding tables to my garage" and "I can host a photo-scanning party and invite all of my photographer friends over to help." I was already rationalizing how I could make this work.

I was once told by a therapist friend that, "No!" is a full sentence. I'm not known for using that sentence very often. After all, being agreeable has led me to some of the most fun adventures of my life. I can't recall how many times I've been on an airplane on a day's notice, or found myself dancing to a live band when I thought I was going to be in bed by 9 pm that same night.

My friend Jen jokingly says, "Krista is so up for anything that you aren't truly her friend until she has convinced you to risk your life for the sake of a fun adventure." And interestingly enough, months down the road, after Lori and I had forged a friendship, I did in fact convince her to leave her comfort zone and *maybe* I put us in some slight danger —Los Angeles, a speakeasy, a dark alley and a password I had gotten from a valet I'd met that morning... All to say, "Yes!" is also a full sentence.

I knew that agreeing to help Lori would be something I'd look back at fondly, even if it meant a lot of work along the way.

I hadn't quite agreed on the undertaking yet before David had gotten Lori on the phone. I'm not sure if she realized, but he had her on speaker and I could hear everything she was saying. He asked her, "Lori, do you know which of these bags is most important?" She began to talk about the different albums, her childhood pictures, her mother's childhood, school pictures, family photographs, photos of her late brother.

I could hear the scratchiness in her voice until she couldn't hold back. She began to sob. I could tell Lori was fighting through tears to get out the words, "I just don't know."

I could feel her pain coming through the phone, just as deeply as if she was standing next to me that day. I irrationally blurted out, "Don't worry, I'll just take all of them." I knew those words were healing to Lori, even if just for a brief moment. I knew I had the power to give her hope, to fix the problem, to make it better. There aren't many times in life that a single sentence can fix something so profoundly, but in that moment I had the words, and by sharing them with Lori I was able to heal some pain. In my heart I had no choice but to say, "Yes! I will fix this."

Lori thanked me profusely as David hung up the phone. I could tell David was happy to have my help too, even if it was just to relieve Lori's pain a little bit. I wasn't exactly sure how I was going to accomplish this monumental task, but I knew I had done the right thing.

David needed to return to the project he was orchestrating in the house, and I had my work cut out for me with their pictures. We made a few trips to my SUV to fill it with the trash bags. I once again spent another afternoon driving home with my windows down in an attempt to combat that familiar moldy smell.

I don't know how many pictures there were in those six trash bags. I never did count them. Jeffery had told me he thought it was about 3,000 pictures. It was definitely the single largest group of photographs I had taken on and was more than enough to keep me busy for a long time. There weren't any regrets in my saying "Yes," though. I was thankful to help Lori and thankful that I had made a new friend in the process.

Ending Chapter Eight
Are your photographs safely stored?

The number one safest solution is to have a digital backup of every photograph, but it's still important to keep your printed photographs as safe as possible.

These are the best practices to care for prints so that they will stand up to the test of time and potential disaster.

Tips for safely storing photographs:

- Do not keep pictures in stacks or in boxes where they are touching each other.
- Put every photograph in an album with sleeves.
- Look for an archival album that is acid-free, lignin-free and that does not contain PVC.
- Avoid albums that are self-adhesive or magnetic.
- A scrapbook-style album using photo corners to attach the photo to a page is a good option, however make sure there is paper or tissue between the photographs so they do not touch each other when the album is closed.
- Keep the albums in a climate-controlled space.

CHAPTER NINE

HOLLYWOOD

Back at the headquarters, aka my kitchen, I began to organize Lori's pictures. I cautiously peeled each photograph from its album, but many of the pages fell apart. Most albums were in pieces by the time I was finished; the remains of each moldy mess would be taken out to the trash. Some weeks I would fill multiple trash cans with scraps of albums like Lori's.

The photographs that I had removed were washed and set out to dry. I would get a digital copy of every one. Some were sent off to the volunteers for restoration, or "extra love," as I would call it.

My assistant, Maddie, and her mom, Jen, both took a large group of pictures to their own homes. Olivia made the two-hour trek home from college, Jess would come over, and even Carrie (a client whom I barely even knew at the time), generously offered to help. I was determined to figure out a way to successfully get through Lori's thousands of pictures.

Many conversations were sparked by the colorful stories told in Lori's images. From a picture of a man, who I was convinced was Ernest Hemingway, fishing sometime in the 1930s, to a photograph of a little girl in the 1980s proudly showing off a Cabbage Patch doll. There was an entire album of military photographs, and the very well documented year the inground pool was installed. Lori and her family had documented a past that spanned several lifetimes.

It was always clear when the family got a new camera, as we would see a shift in the type of images. Luckily, Lori's family really embraced the Polaroid camera in the 1970s and '80s; those pictures might just be bulletproof. I had spent so much time carefully peeling apart photographs that had stuck together and trying to restore images where the ink had smeared away, but the Polaroids—they stood up to that hurricane. Most were as good as new. I consistently advise people to backup their pictures and to make digital copies. But if there is to only be one photograph, the Polaroid is definitely the most indestructible.

Over the next couple of months, I would send Lori regular text messages with photo updates; a restored photograph of a special moment she likely hadn't seen in years would be a little something positive for her day. Pictures of her adult son as a little boy, photographs of her late grandparents, sweet memories that would pop into her text messages with just a little bit of brightness. I knew she needed it too. It wasn't much, but just a little bit of something that I hoped would help her get through a dark time.

The day I returned the first group of Lori's photos to her was one I'll never forget. It was a Saturday afternoon. She came to my house with her mom, Patty, and son, Jeffery. They arrived with pizza and soda for everyone. This was actually the first time that I had met Lori in person, but we had a text message relationship that had already bonded us. We were there so she could simply get her restored photographs, but the vibe was more like we had all arrived for a huge celebration. The moment she walked in the door I gave her the biggest hug as Lori said, "My angel!", the nickname she had lovingly given me.

Scott and my friend Jess joined for pizza. They had both helped me with Lori's photographs and now we were all getting to know the faces that up till then we had only seen in the pictures.

There were a lot of laughs as we got to know each other. Until that day, it seemed like every conversation revolved around suffering, but this was different. Lori and I had already had the difficult conversations, and I think we were all tired of the heartache. We all wanted a little slice of "normal." So there we sat, the six of us, squeezed around a table for four that I had cleared of pictures just for the occasion. It was a simple thing, pizza with new friends, but it was exactly what my heart needed.

We finished our pizza and moved over to my dining room, where I had spread out the hundreds of restored pictures across the table. Together, we looked at every single photo. I was nervous to show Lori the ones I wasn't able to save. I knew there would be some sadness over those. Many of the photographs of her late brother. Just gone forever. I could feel a lump in my throat as I pointed to what remained of those pictures, the ones where there was no hope. I know she was sad about those photographs. Her brother was a child in the '60s, back when every moment wasn't captured. There were so few images of him, and so many were gone. Pictures hold our memories, they keep loved ones close even when they are not. I can only imagine what it must have felt like to know those pictures were lost forever.

Those brief moments of sadness were far exceeded by happy gasps of joy as they each looked at the successfully restored photographs. Lori's mom had thought that everything had gone in the trash. To her, seeing her memories spread across my dining room table was a huge and welcome surprise.

We spent almost the entire day going over those pictures. Patty would pick up each photo, one at a time, and share a little insight into each moment. She laughed as she picked up a childhood photo of her husband. "This was TJ when he was sent off to boarding school," she said. Apparently, he was a mischievous child and she found a lot of humor in that photo and memory.

Patty is a spunky 86-year-old woman with a very quick wit. She had funny commentary for each photo, quick to say if there was a family member she wasn't too fond of or to share a crazy thing she did in her youth. It was like watching a stand up comedy routine, and she nailed every joke. I am sure that day was the most I had laughed in months.

It was the photographs that kept these stories alive for Patty. They inspired memories that she may have otherwise forgotten, and funny stories we may have never heard. The photos provided the person, the place, the moment, or the feeling she had when it was taken. And she shared it all.

Before they left that day, Patty gave me one of her photographs to keep. It sits on my desk now as a reminder of the entire project. It's a photo of Patty's Uncle Bud.

When I was working on their pictures, that particular photograph really stuck out to me. It was a 1940s hand-painted photograph of a young man in military fatigues. It wasn't a formal photograph, like so many other military pictures. This one was casual, depicting the man's profile. This one wasn't taken in a studio like the others I'd encountered, this one was outside and more candid. I had mentioned to Patty and Lori that it had an artistic quality that I loved. Patty then took the photo out of the piles of pictures and handed it to me. She said, "You will get more enjoyment out of this one than I will, I don't need it anymore." She graciously gave me that photo of Uncle Bud.

Bud Herbst from Pittsburgh, Pennsylvania. I mostly look at the photo and imagine the life he led, but Google gave me a few answers too. He served in the U.S. Navy as a Seabee during WWII, was married for 62 years, and had children, grandchildren, and great grandchildren before he passed away in 2013.

I wonder about the moment that photo was taken. Could he have imagined then that a stranger, who was yet to be born for another 30-some years, would eventually display that picture on her desk? That photo has value to me today, but I'm sure in a very different way than it did to Bud back in 1945, when he likely mailed it home to his parents.

That photo of Uncle Bud left me with so many questions. Perhaps its thought-provoking quality is one of the things I love about it. Mostly, it makes me wonder where all of our photos will end up? Will my pictures ever land on a stranger's desk?

I happily accepted the offer to keep Uncle Bud. Then I helped Lori and Patty gather the rest of the photographs. I also gave Lori all of the digital files from the scans I had made. They were all backed up and organized. Each could be enjoyed as a print or on their computers and phones. Now, their most valued possessions were properly secured.

It was bittersweet to watch the mountains of pictures that had filled my home go back to where they belonged. In total, we had spent five hours looking over them all, but the time flew. We all said our good-byes and off they went.

The next time I saw Lori, we were boarding a plane in Fort Myers, headed for Los Angeles. Olivia joined us, and the three of us went off on an unforgettable adventure. One that proved to be a most epic and so needed girls trip.

Interviews and news coverage had become a regular thing, but I did get one call that really stuck out. It was a producer for *The Kelly Clarkson Show*. She said that Kelly wanted to do a zoom-style interview with me, along with a person I had helped. I immediately gave her Lori's information. The producer spoke to Lori and they hit it off; Lori befriends everyone she meets, so I wasn't surprised in the least. *The Kelly Clarkson Show* then decided against the zoom interview, and asked instead to fly us both to Los Angeles to actually be on the show.

We made our way from LAX to Hollywood via a blacked-out SUV they sent for us and a driver who had likely never been asked so many "tell me about this celebrity" questions in his life.

When we arrived at Universal Studios, we were given a swanky greenroom, got to meet the celebrity guests, Toheeb Jimoh and Nicole Byer, and, of course, meet THE Kelly Clarkson. The show is taped in a studio that had the feeling of sitting right in Kelly's living room. However, looking out at the live audience and seeing the dozens of cameras brought us right back to reality. When it was our turn to tape we had a brief moment to chat with Kelly, but then in what felt like record time we were taping.

After hours of anticipation leading up to the taping, the 10 minutes we actually sat on that stage felt like the blink of an eye. We grabbed a few photos with Kelly, Toheeb, and Nicole, and then joined Olivia in the greenroom. We likely left that studio a little more excited than your average talk show guest. We cheered and celebrated as if we had just wrapped up opening night in a Broadway show.

To commemorate our adventure on *The Kelly Clarkson Show*, I organized the most epic Hollywood-style "night on the town." Restaurants that offered foods decoratively presented in minuscule portions and bars with fancy martinis served by mixologists were all on the agenda.

But there was more! Because, as we've established, with me, there's always more. Olivia and I decided to surprise Lori with a stop at a posh speakeasy. Lori later admitted she thought we were trying to break into a rundown building, but I'm glad she shares my love of adventure, because it really did turn into the best night ever. We partied till almost midnight that night, which, in our defense, was 3 am, our time. It was one of the best nights of my life, and I'm sure Lori and Olivia (whom Lori now lovingly refers to as her niece) would most definitely agree. Another bright spot that came from unfortunate circumstances, damaged pictures, and a "Yes!"

When we returned from Los Angeles, Lori's house had just been completed and was ready for her to move back in. In total it took six months to rebuild. New floors, new walls, all new furnishings and appliances were installed. The begging to contractors and the pleading with insurance had finally come to an end. That painful chapter was closed, and I was so happy to see her finally be home.

Lori still sends me sweet messages and checks in from time to time. Her kindness continues to be a light in my life. She still calls me her angel, although I think she's just as much mine. It was her pictures that filled my kitchen and gave me purpose. It was her genuine friendship that filled my heart when my heart needed it the most. I have no doubt that Lori coming into my life was a gift from God.

Ending Chapter Nine

Are you ready to begin securing and organizing your pictures? Start today with these easy steps:

- Download a photo scanning app like PhotoMyne, Google PhotoScan and / or purchase an at-home photo scanner to get the highest quality scan
- Purchase a photo album to place those loose pictures in.
- Mark a time on your calendar that is set aside for photo organizing.
- Talk with friends or family and schedule a time to make it a group effort.
- Set aside a little time each week to work on the project, don't do too much at once.
- Make a list of where all of your photographs are located.
- Do other family members have some? Your own childhood pictures, your significant others childhood pictures, photographs of ancestors? Try to collect all of those pictures.
- Think about your digital pictures too. Do you have old phones and computers that have pictures stored on them? The goal is to get all of the pictures living together in one organized location.
- Begin the process of gathering all of those photographs.

CHAPTER TEN

SANIBEL ISLAND

The first time I drove over the causeway to Sanibel Island was in 1997, just before I had officially moved to Florida. I still remember my first impression of the sleepy town. It wasn't like the Jersey Shore where I had grown up spending summers, actually it was the complete opposite. It was quiet and unassuming. There were no big monuments and no high-rises. There were no water parks, and not a single putt-putt course to be found. My 21-year-old brain had already decided what a beach community looked like, and this most certainly was not it.

It was instead an "in bed by 9 pm" sort of town. One that had a very unique charm that quickly found a special place in my heart. It was the nature that got me—lots of nature, actually. And the community embraced that pristine, natural setting. Large pockets of land are preserved to this day, and even the developed areas boast landscaping with native plants so lush that you wonder, "is there actually a house back there?"

The beaches are easy to fall in love with too. I recall the first time I saw massive piles of sea shells pushed up along the shoreline and thought I'd stumbled across a hidden treasure. My eyes were glued to the ground as I admired what could have been billions of shells. Those piles stretched on for miles, and I quickly learned it was an everyday occurrence, just another thing that makes Sanibel so special.

Though arguably, the best part of Sanibel is that even when the place is packed on a holiday weekend, you can still manage to find privacy. You don't have to take too far a walk down the beach to find yourself isolated from the world. Your own quiet oasis is always a few steps away.

I don't live on Sanibel, but I definitely call it my community. I was a regular volunteer at several of the island's nonprofits, my photographs are often in the local newspaper, and you can grab my business card at the Welcome Center; it really is like a second home to me.

When Hurricane Ian took its toll on Sanibel Island, it hurt as much as if it were my own neighborhood. The storm surge took out many of the iconic island spots; restaurants and parks that were loved by everyone, just gone. I later read an estimate that one in ten structures on the 12-mile-long island were demolished, not to mention so many more that were severely damaged. Estimates of up to 15 feet of flood water covered the island. Naturally, every one of its 6,000 residents was impacted.

Today, many of those places that I once loved sit as empty lots. Most people I know have left the island, some so they can rebuild, the rest are gone forever. The wedding venues where I loved reporting to work, all closed. And no, not "mostly" closed—*all*—all closed, nearly two years later.

My friends that I'd chat with at the various venues were, for the most part, let go from their jobs. Casa Ybel, the resort where Jessica, JoAnne, and José would greet us with the biggest smiles, remains closed. I used to see José every week, but haven't heard from him since the storm. JoAnne later told me there is nothing you can do to prepare yourself to lose your house, your car, and your job all at once, but that was her reality. Jessica, who had been with the rsort for 20 years, was in the same situation. She relocated to another state. Left the area forever.

Under normal circumstances, there would have been a big going away party for Jessica—we are in the event industry, after all. And everyone loved Jessica. I am positive my friend Jana would have created giant floral centerpieces, and Steve would have been strumming his guitar as dozens of island-wedding professionals would flock to thank her for her tireless work in the industry. Those life-changing mashed potatoes would be passed in tiny hors d'oeuvres cups, or at least I would've strongly suggested it. Maddie and I would be there, taking pictures of Jessica with every guest as if she was Mickey Mouse at Disney World. Toasts to Jessica, and her years in the wedding industry, would likely go on for way too long. With everything she had done to make Sanibel Island weddings so spectacular, I know that every person in that room would want a turn on the microphone. It would have been an epic celebration to honor an incredible person.

Unfortunately, there was no going away party for Jessica. It was months later before I heard the rumor that she had moved away. We had been a part of hundreds of weddings together, and that had officially come to an end in the most abrupt way. It was unfortunate that we never got to have a going away party, really unfortunate I never even got the opportunity to say goodbye.

Months would go by before I even got to see the destruction that happened to Casa Ybel. Sanibel was closed to nonresidents.

Even though I wasn't doing my daily photoshoots on Sanibel, I'd still find myself almost instinctively attempt to navigate in its direction when I'd get in my car. Almost like my soul just wanted to be there, sitting peacefully on the beach watching the last of a sunset, or collecting one more shell. It'll likely be years before that is again a daily routine, and it'll most definitely never be the same.

Although I couldn't drive over to Sanibel Island, I was still able to help several island residents with their damaged photographs. Each would make the trek off island to my house so we could get together and exchange photos.

It was those Sanibel Island residents that brought the largest variety of pictures: a framed portrait with President Bill Clinton, a family photo that stood four feet tall, a collection of antique car photographs. Buried in one box was the cover of a 2005 golf magazine that had been carefully cut out and framed, although I never did learn what its importance was. Each one was dropped off with hopes that I could save them.

Denise was one of the Sanibel residents that came to me. She had seen my work in a news story and reached out, asking if I could look at the damaged photographs she had been holding on to. I agreed and invited her over.

Like so many others, she thought her photographs were safe before the storm and had never considered that they were at risk. They were stored in a tote on a shelf in her closet, where they had been for years. She never counted on gargantuan amounts of flood water rushing through her home.

Before the storm Denise had evacuated, leaving for what was planned to be a two-day stay at a hotel on the other coast. Two weeks would pass before she could access Sanibel again, but she already knew its fate. The entire island had been under water and the news footage made it clear, nothing in her 6,000 resident community was left unscathed.

Denise knew her beloved Sanibel home was left in what looked like a war zone, but nothing prepared her for that first trip back. Debris covered every roadway. The roads themselves were destroyed, the asphalt broken apart and washed away as if it was made of pebbles. Animal carcasses were lying among the debris and the few bits of nature that stayed rooted in the ground were brown and dead.

She made her way back to her home, hopeful that it was among the few that were still livable. She quickly learned that was not the case. Although still standing, it wasn't a sight she was prepared to face. Her beautiful home looked as though it was turned upside down, coated with sludge, and put back down. Just attempting to open the doors was a feat. When she finally got inside it was complete devastation. Two weeks of mold had covered what was an already disastrous scene, making the environment toxic and the smell unbearable.

That tote that she had carefully stored her pictures in couldn't stand up to the destruction of the storm. It was found sitting among the wreckage. Everything around it was destroyed and she could tell at a glance, the pictures inside were likely destroyed too.

That first day at her home was one of many difficult trips. She would leave her hotel at 3 am, take the long drive back to her house and work on it until it was dark. It was months before she had running water or electricity, making the necessary clean up dangerous and challenging.

During one of her trips back, Denise brought me her photographs. When she arrived at my house several weeks had passed since the storm, and it was obvious she was emotionally beaten down. The pain of the loss, and the weeks of aggravation that followed had taken a toll on her. I could tell she was trying to be polite, to be positive, to keep her composure. Though that facade was thinly veiled. I could see she was hurting and it didn't take long before everything began to come out.

The scratched and beaten tote that she hadn't found the courage to even open yet sat in front of us on my kitchen counter. She specifically listed a few important photographs she knew were in it, but much of its exact contents were still unknown. She was too afraid to see the memories that likely were all destroyed.

For Denise, having someone to open that box with her was as important as saving the photographs themselves. In that moment, I am positive she would have happily selected a root canal over the destruction that she was likely about to face. This particular loss was different from the record collection, the cloth napkin sets, and old text books that had likely all been thrown away by now. This was the one loss she was putting off facing because she knew it would hurt the most.

I could see her eyes begin to well up as I slowly took the lid off of the box. I maintained my usual, super peppy, "keep it positive" routine, but this time it was with a lump in my throat. The stakes were high. Denise was fragile. And another loss would be unbearable.

We stood in my kitchen and one by one, we pulled apart the soggy mess. First to come out of the box was a stack of old greeting cards that she had received over the years. They were still wet, crinkled, and had some moldy spots on them already. At this point, Denise was no longer holding back the tears. She sobbed as she said to me, "I guess they are destroyed."

I did my best to assure her. "No, no, they are fine," I told her, "You are going to take your phone and take a photograph of each one. Then you will have it forever." I think that did offer her some relief.

The cards were filled with beautiful sentiments that had been shared with her over the years. Clearly Denise was very loved, there were so many kind messages that understandably she would want to keep. I told her, "You'll always have those messages and now they can live on your phone and your computer so you can read them anytime."

Denise needed good news. I was so thankful that the greeting card situation was resolved. One tiny win. Then we moved on to the things that I knew might not have such an easy solution.

I placed rows of paper towels down across my kitchen counters, and then began to spread out the contents of the box. There were a few pictures that had miraculously survived without a single mark. That wasn't the case with most of them though. Many were in stacks that were completely stuck together, dried in a clump as solid as a brick. We could only see the lone photograph on top of each hardened, stuck-together stack. Her wedding photographs, honeymoon pictures, and a retirement party were all hidden in that mess.

Pictures all cemented together were a common finding as I was working on the hurricane-damaged photographs. It actually doesn't take a flood for that to happen either. Humidity and dampness can do it too. Once the pictures are exposed to any damp conditions, and then dry in a stack, they will often stick to the photographs they are piled with. When they are completely dried they are like a brick. The group becomes a rock solid block. When you try to pull them apart the photographic paper can tear, and the image can be destroyed. That can be one of the hardest situations to restore. I knew that I had my work cut out for me with Denise and her pictures.

When Denise walked into my house that day, before we had even gotten to the box, she immediately began to share regrets. She mentioned how she had intended to put these pictures in albums and wished she had stored them somewhere higher. They had lived in that box for years. They were a future project in the "when I have time" category. There likely was always something more pressing, and that future project never did happen.

As we stood in my kitchen, pulling out photographs with orange speckled salt water stains and smeared ink blotches, she continued to blame herself. "If I had just organized this box earlier," she said, as she tried again to hold back tears. That really struck a deep chord in me. She was blaming herself in a situation that was completely out of her control. I had only met Denise minutes earlier, but I was ready to go to any length to take this pain away from her. I wanted to wave a magic wand, and make those photographs reappear all neatly presented in the album that she intended for them. I still wasn't sure how many of her photos I would be able to fix, but I knew I was going to do everything in my power to bring back as many as possible.

Denise apologetically continued to explain how this happened, but the more she did, the more my heart just hurt for her. She was not alone, and I reassured her that it was not her fault. Everyone has a box of pictures that they have good intentions for. Those old memories that live in the closet with the "when I have more time" earmark. I had heard this same story from so many people. Photographs in the storage unit, in a box in the garage, in the back of the closet; they weren't displayed prominently in their homes, but they still were described as the most painful loss. Regrets were always among the conversations I had with people—regrets of not having gotten digital copies, regrets of not taking their pictures when they left... even the painful regrets of not evacuating at all.

As I talked with Denise, and so many others in the same situation, I realized that part of the procrastination in never getting digital scans of pictures was in not knowing how. I hesitated in immediately sharing how easy that could have been, a bit of salt in the wound. But if only Denise had known there was an app for her phone that would have helped her, and quickly, it could have entirely changed her circumstances. It's not as complicated as anyone thinks, and it's so easy to prevent this heartache.

I gave Denise the biggest hug. It was the kind of embrace that in the past I would have reserved for my closest friends in the midst of a crisis. But it was the only thing I could offer to ease any of her pain.

Her entire life had been disrupted. It wasn't just the loss of her home; it was the loss of her community, her daily routine, her sense of purpose, all gone in the same moment. The stories she shared with me weren't epic struggles, trying to escape rushing water like many others. Our conversations were simply about her just trying to live on.

She had already taken the big blows, now she was consumed by trying to get by each day. Where is the mail going, and when will she be able to cook in a kitchen again? Those were the conversations we had. Simple things, almost trivial in some ways, but the reality was, just living was now difficult.

Everywhere Denise looked, everywhere she went, was riddled with painful reminders. Living in a hotel room where the first sight she'd wake up to was boxes of disorganized personal items piled next to the bed; it had to have been jarring. How could she even begin to heal when it was still all around her? I had listened to so many stories of surviving the day of the storm, but the things Denise shared will forever change how I look at the victims of disaster. Surviving that first day is a small part of *living* through it.

Denise and I stood in my kitchen for an hour or two. There was a lot of pain in opening that box, but I think she left that day feeling a little better about it. She had lost so much, I promised her this was one loss that we were going to try to fix.

She left me with a pile of pictures, and a big job. I got to work, uncovering what was stuck together, digitizing what was damaged, and piecing back together what I could.

I scanned each photo and sent the digital images off to Miss Toto's class in Connecticut. They too quickly got to work on her pictures. The students felt a special connection to Denise right away. I would get messages asking, "How is Denise doing?" I could see how her vibrant smile in those old photographs could make you feel like you knew her, even though the students had never spoken to her before. They genuinely cared about her, and were putting the most effort they could into her photographs. That effort was visible, as one by one, each photo was sent back to me in beautiful, restored condition.

Nearly a year would pass before Denise and I met up again. Her photographs had been carefully restored months earlier but coming back to collect them wasn't that easy for her. Her time spent back in the area was consumed by the work on her house, and her living situation, hours away, was still temporary with little space to store anything.

Reuniting Denise with her restored photographs was emotional. This time it was tears of joy as she saw long forgotten memories uncovered from those solid stacks she had entrusted me with. Her home was still a work in progress, and things were still far from "normal," but her memories, the ones she feared were gone, were put back together.

The Sanibel community is also still a work in progress. One year after the storm, less than 25% of the residents were able to return to their homes and an even smaller percentage of the island businesses had reopened. Most of the 30 plus hotels, inns and cottages that once made the island a tourist destination, continued to remain closed. However, many of those properties are diligently trudging along, with plans to reopen by the end of 2024. Although some are closed and gone forever.

It may be a long time before every structure is restored, but my favorite part of the island made the quickest comeback. Mother Nature was the first to rebuild. Most of the vegetation had regained its tropical beauty within a few months. One summer of growth and beautiful greens began to refill the no longer baron space. The beaches welcomed back the lush sea grass, and those magical shells have since continued to pile up on the shoreline. Today you can sit on the beach, look out at the water and never know the epic tragedy it was a part of such a short time ago.

A drive that used to be part of my daily routine is now taken just once or twice a month. That causeway that was once a beautiful scene from a postcard is a construction zone, lined with concrete barriers protecting cars from filthy dirt piles and dusty machinery; a project that is due to continue into 2025. I still head over there though, making my way to the beach to meet the few people who still want to capture a beautiful island portrait. And once I'm back on the path to the beach, walking through the regrown sea grass, heading towards that turquoise water, I'm back with the Sanibel that I fell in love with, more thankful than ever.

Ending Chapter Ten
Are you procrastinating?

Tips to avoid procrastination

- Out of sight out of mind - bring those pictures out of the closet.
- If you have the space, create a photo organizing area in your home.
- Pull some old photo albums out to enjoy now and to remind you to start your mission!
- Set a scheduled time to work on photo-organizing.
- Join a photo-organizing group for inspiration and accountability.
- Don't look at it as a large overwhelming project, it can be more easily accomplished in small increments.
- Don't put pressure on yourself if you don't always get through a lot of pictures. It's okay to stop and enjoy those old memories too.
- Remember, future you will be thankful this is accomplished!
- And, future generations will benefit from your efforts now too!

CHAPTER ELEVEN

NORTH FORT MYERS

The neighborhood where Kaye's father lived was one of the worst sights I'd ever seen. First off, it's huge. I've been to that house in North Fort Myers several times, but I don't think I could ever find my way back to it without GPS. It's a seemingly endless maze of streets, and it was lined with houses that had been totally flooded. The sheer magnitude of the level of destruction will always be stuck in my head.

It was my passion for compassion that brought me back to that neighborhood. It was also that passion that led me to knock on strangers doors. And that's how I met Rosie.

Down the street and around the bend from Kaye's fathers home is a salmon colored stucco house, with several palm trees in the front yard. A home that exudes Floridian. It was clear when I got to it though, that it had seen better days. The garage door was gone, replaced by sheets of plywood. The street was lined with enough refuse to have filled up multiple moving trucks: a couch, a mattress, cabinetry with a giant tattered and bent patio umbrella across the top, along with so many other things that I couldn't even identify. Pieces and parts and broken things. As I approached the front door it was propped open, and before I could even knock I was greeted by a tiny white dog, and a voice shouting over the sound of several blowing fans, "Come on in."

I could already see through the open doorway that the walls were all torn apart, exposing the wooden framing throughout the house. This was a gorgeous home, with a big dining area and large open rooms. I imagined that many celebrations took place there, it had the feel of a home that was meant for entertaining. And Floridians do like their entertaining. I imagined this home was that kind of spot where people would gather, but it definitely took all the imagination I could muster. Presently, it was in complete disarray. Cabinetry and walls were all torn apart. Makeshift furniture covered with cleaning supplies and tools stood in place of the tattered, mocha leather couch and broken coffee table that now sat out on the curb.

You know how some people are like old friends before you even get to know them? That's Rosie, with everyone. She is bubbly and charming and exudes that Florida hospitality that you can't help but love. When I walked up to Rosie's house she wasn't expecting me and had no idea why I was even there, but before I had a chance to explain, she was inviting me into her home. I'm pretty sure she even offered me a drink before I could introduce myself.

When I did finally get to explain why I had stopped by, she was taken aback by my offer to help. "Well that's just wonderful," she exclaimed. "Yes! I do have photographs that were damaged."

Rosie stands not much more than five feet tall. Although petite, her presence is large. She is a spunky woman with a big smile and a warmth that you can immediately feel. Her positive energy and zest for life are definitely contagious. And lucky me, by some grace of God I was standing in her kitchen, very happy to be soaking in some of her radiant joy.

After a few laughs and some light conversation, Rosie took me to locate the photographs she had set aside. She led me to a small back room where stacks of miscellaneous household things were left in seemingly unorganized piles. Rubbermaid totes were spread throughout the room. This was the room they had designated to collect the things they could possibly salvage. It looked like a scene from the

TV show *Hoarders*, but it was obvious that given the circumstances, this chaos was only out of necessity and urgency.

They were the things Rosie still had hope for, her photographs included. There wasn't anywhere near a household's worth, but just enough that it took her a little digging to find the pictures. She sighed as she pulled out a photo album. I could tell this was particularly concerning to her. She held up a soggy, water-logged album and said, "Can we do anything about this?" It wasn't in the best shape, but I knew there were definitely pictures that could be restored. She kept finding more pictures and handed each to me until my arms were full.

We moved to an empty room where we could spread the photographs out. This room was in the back of her house. It had a view out to a beautiful palm tree lined canal. I could imagine better days spent there, looking out to the water, watching the tropical birds fly by. Now we sat on the floor, listening to those fans humming and looking out at the disarray that once was a peaceful view.

As we sat there, Rosie began to tell me of the terror of that day, when the hurricane hit. She and her husband didn't evacuate. They stayed in their house and watched as the water came into their home. Their house is two stories, so they were able to escape the flood water by staying upstairs. But as the water kept rising, they weren't sure that would be safe. They watched down the staircase as everything they owned began to float by. The quaint canal their home sits on rose until it met the neighboring river, essentially putting them in the middle of their combined force.

Their home isn't near the beach or the Gulf of Mexico, like some that had seen the storm surge. This house is 20 miles from the gulf.

This area wasn't like the tourist-filled beach communities where I would go to do beach photo shoots. This neighborhood was all local residents, everyday people. Likely teachers, police officers, mechanics, and nurses.

Rosie shared with me that many of the residents tried to escape as the water began to rise, but it rose too fast and quickly became too deep to drive through. Rosie said the streets were filled with flooded cars that were abandoned during the storm as people attempted to get out. I recall how terrified I was during the storm, thinking we may have to run to our neighbors home to take cover. The wind was so powerful, and large debris flew through the air like pieces of paper. My neighbors live so close that we can almost hold a conversation while each standing in our own garage, but yet the idea of making that sprint was terrifying. I can only imagine the horror of trying to flee by car only to find yourself in rapidly rising water. I wondered back to the dog I had seen on a leash in the canal. Could that dog have been part of one of those failed escapes?

Rosie shared many details of that day, but would always turn it back to something positive. Her and her husband were rebuilding their home themselves, doing a lot of clean up, demolition, and construction with little help from others. She would share a story of something that was ruined but quickly would talk of how they were able to rebuild it or managed to find a perfectly fine replacement. They continued to live in the house, occupying only the upstairs bedroom. It had to have been hard to never be able to escape the damages and reminders of that terror. But their staying only serves as a testament to Rosie's optimism. The only tears I've ever seen her shed were tears of joy when she would later see her restored images.

Rosie and I sat there together on that floor, going photo by photo, talking about how much each meant to her. A black and white photograph of her husband's college football team was destroyed. The muddy water pulled the ink off the picture till it was almost unrecognizable, there was really nothing we could do to fix that one. She was disappointed, but we focused on the ones we could fix. There were too many opportunities all around us to be sad, my goal was to bring hope and get smiles. With Rosie, that was easy.

There were definitely a lot of pictures that could be saved. I offered to take them with me that day. Rosie was so happy, she hugged me like we were old friends. I do think of her as an old friend now. The friend who I met under some unusual and tragic circumstances, but a great friend nonetheless.

We stood in the doorway and continued to talk before I left with her pictures. I think she may have appreciated the excuse to get away from the constant clean up for just a few minutes longer. And there definitely was some normalcy in chatting with a new friend, I could appreciate that too.

As I left that day, I passed by Kaye's fathers house. The team of volunteers and friends were all gone now. They had done all they could do for that now vacant home. Kaye's husband, Jim, was there alone, finishing up a few last clean up projects. It was a shell of a house. The cabinetry and flooring were all gone, and there wasn't a single item remaining. Kaye's brother's home, several hours away, was where her dad would reside for now. It was decided that her dad would never go back to North Fort Myers or his home. That chapter was closed. A sign now sat behind the debris: "For Sale As is."

I continued my drive back out through that endlessly winding neighborhood and made my way home. I was going back to the quiet solitude of restoring pictures. I had taken Rosie's soggy album with me along with a few others I had collected that day. Rosie didn't give me as many pictures as Lori or Denise, but these were just as important to her.

There were photographs of her children, her late mother, and her trip to Israel. It wasn't an overwhelming pile of pictures, it was the kind of small group you would happily pass down for generations. I could see her grandchildren enjoying having any of these sweet treasures handed to them. They were the kind of pictures that came with great stories. Nothing like the overwhelming and sometimes mundane pictures we keep on our phones today. There was no screenshot of a grocery list or photo of a pair of shoes that she never did buy. These were important pictures, and I was on a mission to save them if not for her, for her grandchildren.

I washed and digitized each photo. I sent the digital files to Peggy in Idaho and Erin in New York and Gina in Wisconsin. A group went to Miss Toto's class in Connecticut too. All were beautifully restored by talented volunteers.

Rosie was among the people who would later zoom with the Amity High School students. I knew her contagious optimism and zest for life would be a hit with the kids, and it was. I watched each student beam with pride as they showed her what they had done. She praised the students, and made them feel so good about their accomplishment, all while shedding tears of joy. I know if she could have met them in person, she would have gone student-by-student to give each one of those 30 kids a hug. You could feel that even through the zoom. I was so glad to see her pictures restored too. What started as a sad album dripping with water, was now pictures that looked better than when they started. I was very proud of the students and so happy for Rosie. She truly deserved this kindness and I fed off of the positivity. There was a lot of work still ahead of me and that day provided the motivation I needed to keep going.

Ending Chapter Eleven
Let's create a heritage folder for your pictures.

Rosie had a small, curated group of photographs that would be perfect to pass down to future generations. Here are ideas for how you can also create a folder to pass down:

- Start a new folder on your computer
- Label it **Heritage Folder**
- Within that folder, start a new folder for every year, go back as far as you can document for your family. Grandparents, great grandparents, include pictures of everyone who is relevant to your family's future generations.
- Add digital photographs of each family member in the year that they were taken.
- Continue this process, adding every year to date.
- For recent years, where thousands of photographs may have been taken, narrow down each year to a small group. As few as 25 per year could be an impactful collection.
- Include clear, camera facing images of each family member. Also include family milestones, births, weddings, graduations, accomplishments.

Using metadata to note important information:

Metadata is the digital equivalent of writing on the back of a photograph. This information is in the digital file and will stay with the photo.

- Open the photo thumbnails on your computer.
- Right click on a photo.
- Mac users select "get info" - PC users select "properties"
- In the window that pops up you will see a blank space for comments or description.
- Write pertinent, identifying information to the photo there.
- Repeat this process for each digital photograph.
- This information will remain with the digital file and is searchable on a computer.
- Save this folder on flash drives and give one to each family member to keep.

CHAPTER TWELVE

HUMPTY DUMPTY

L ori's, Denise's, and Rosie's stories were just a few of the many I would hear. Their photographs were among the thousands that would pass through my home.

However, happy to say, eventually, there were no more pictures to wash. Though there was plenty still to be done.

Scott was happy to see the piles of pictures now relegated to just the dining room. Maddie was still stopping by, and Olivia was making trips back from college to help me digitize pictures, but it was a much less involved process now. What was once a photo-saving factory operating as smoothly as a Chick-fil-A over the lunch hour had now become a mundane process as I would simply digitize and send off each photograph for Photoshop restoration.

Many people had painstakingly dried and cleaned every one of their photographs themselves. They then set their damaged picture aside as they addressed more pressing things. It would be over a year before some would finally reach out, but when they did I would still hear the stories of their hurricane struggles. It wasn't as raw as it was in the first weeks after the storm. In those initial days, stories were told through tears, many with such distinct details. Now, those panicked stories had passed; now people spoke in facts. Maybe they had become numb to the pain, or perhaps it was just that the story had been told so many times. I wonder if it began to feel like sharing the story of Humpty Dumpty, recounting someone else's story with little emotional attachment. A story that would be told in the same way, with the same factual details, every single time.

I found myself starting to feel similarly as I spoke about my photo-salvaging efforts. Reporters and news stations had taken a liking to my "good news" story, and I had been repeating the same sound bites over and over again for months. I remember getting a call from Steve Hart-man's producer at the CBS Evening News. I was quick to tell them, "I can connect you with people who are actually saving lives if you want?" I suppose that likely came off as disinterest, I never did hear from them again. All the same, there was no shortage of other news programs eager to chat about my work.

All cards on the table, I was actually embarrassed by the news coverage. My friends had gone into homes checking for survivors, they took their boats to rescue people, they passed out meals, and volunteered at shelters. What did my friends think of my happy little story being splattered all over the news? I continued to do the interviews though. I knew that each interview could mean connecting with one more person who needed help.

And there were always people in need of help, even if the urgency was less. One of those people was my friend Lauren. Her parents' home was severely damaged, and she had collected all of their water-logged photographs. She reached out to me to ask for advice, wanting to know what steps she should take to salvage them. Like so many others at that time, Lauren gave me a factual run down of their unfortunate situation. They were words she had likely shared on repeat, not unlike the very factual explanation I offered her to restore those photographs.

She is an avid photographer too, so she was ready to take on the project herself. I coached her through the work to save the pictures. We talked for an hour or so, mostly photo talk, some catching up, but it wasn't until the end of the conversation that she mentioned in passing that both her and her husband, Michael, had lost their cars to flood water.

So many times throughout those months, I'd think to myself, "if this happened on a normal day it would be a big deal." A friend and her husband both having their cars destroyed on the same day is something that would definitely be talked about in my house. It would be the first thing to come up when Scott would walk in the door after work. "You'll never believe this, Lauren's and Michael's cars were both totaled. Flood water. It destroyed them." I am pretty sure that it didn't even make the line up for our dinner conversation that evening. Funny, as I type out these words, I imagine this will be the first Scott will even know of this.

Lauren and Michael likely incurred a huge cost from their insurance deductible, and it must have been hard to find a new car when so many people were in the same position. I've seen reports that as many as 350,000 cars were all damaged during the storm. This had to have caused them great difficulty, but Lauren didn't mention any of that. Instead, she just said how lucky they were, a sentiment I still hear from people everyday. In a time when incomprehensible loss was everywhere, I'm sure Lauren thought the loss of their cars was trivial. And it was. The shingles off my roof, the landscaping destroyed in my yard, the scare we had when it was all happening– simultaneously terrible and trivial.

There definitely is something about a disaster that puts life into perspective. I found the importance I placed on all sorts of things had most definitely shifted since the hurricane. Yes, there were some things, like listening to a groomsmen toast a couple for their perseverance in relocating a wedding that were now infuriating. However, the vast majority of events were no longer worth fretting over.

My conversation with Lauren has always stuck with me. Her parents were living with her in her apartment, their lives had been turned upside down. Yet, she didn't complain. She was just thankful they had all survived. She shared with me that her parents insisted, "Things can be replaced." And most all of them can be.

She worked hard to restore the photographs for her parents. Even though I wasn't directly involved in that success story, I was still so happy to hear that she was able to get many of her family and childhood photographs restored. Pain and loss had dominated so many conversations before then. This victory, the recovery of something not lost forever, was one of the conversations that I was so very happy to have.

It was the success stories, the ones where photographs were saved and I got to hand a person their cherished memories back, that motivated me to keep going. While initial meetings and first phone calls often seemed numb and robotic, it was the moments where people were reunited with their restored pictures, those were always incredibly emotional. Each time would remind me that photographs are so much more than a piece of paper. For so many, photographs serve as a connection to the past. They offer a window into the lives of our ancestors, family members, and loved ones who are no longer with us. They bring back fond memories of childhood, special occasions, and important milestones too.

After holding onto two severely water-damaged photographs for months, a mother reached out to me. She was devastated that her two sons' high school senior pictures had been destroyed. She kept the scratched and crumpled remnants, thinking that she would eventually need to part with them. Like so many others, she was completely unaware of the power of a skilled Photoshop expert. I know just sharing the words, "I think we can fix these," was enough to have made her day.

When that proud momma brought me those special photographs, she was eager to share the stories of her sons. These men are now grown, and are off doing great things. "One is living abroad, the other a minister in a church," she explained. Of course the last pictures of their time as high school students meant the world to her.

I imagine they are photographs her grandchildren will someday be curious about. Maybe they will look at them and ask, "Do I look like Dad when he was in high school?"

I recall when Olivia first saw my college sorority composite photograph. You know, the ones with the black velvet robe and the boring, drab backdrop? They aren't the most interesting pictures, but they are quite timeless. So timeless, I'm pretty sure they haven't changed their aesthetic in 50 years. Outside of some unusual hairstyles and blue eyeshadow, there are many composite pictures that even I would be hard pressed to date. Is it 1987 or 2019? I know there are some that would be nearly impossible to guess. And apparently, my own Delta Phi Epsilon 1997 sorority composite, where I too donned that black velvet robe, is among those.

Almost 25 years later, Olivia was off to college and joined a sorority of her own. That Greek life tradition lives on, and she had her own composite photograph taken. Around the same time I had been up to visit my family in Pennsylvania. On this visit I dove into an old box of sorority memories that had been stored there for years. Among the treasures was an old strip of composite proofs. Carefully, I sandwiched the strip between cardboard pieces I had cut from a cheerio box in the recycling bin, packed it in my carry-on tote bag and brought it back to Florida with me. Placing the photo on my desk, I had the intention of digitizing it and adding it to my photo collection. Of all of the photographs I have of myself, I definitely wasn't bothered to see this one sitting there everyday. It brought me back to my college adventures, my old friends, and easier times. And, to be honest, seeing myself 40 pounds lighter and wrinkle-free was kinda nice too.

A few weeks later, Olivia had come home from college for a quick visit. As soon as she arrived, she made her way back to my home office. Before I could even stand up to give her a hug, she shouted, "MOM! How did you get my sorority photo?!" I had no idea what she was talking about. I looked across my desk at the piles of random work photographs that I had spread out for the day. Nothing.

I literally had to ask, "What are you talking about?"

She pointed to the far corner of my workspace. "*My* photo!" she said.

I immediately started laughing, she had thought that the 1997 photograph of me was actually of her. I picked it up and handed it to her so she could investigate it closer. It took a moment before she realized what exactly I found so funny. Then she burst out laughing too. It was a solid two minutes of us cracking up before either of us could stop long enough to complete a full sentence.

Olivia had recently been photographed for her composite picture but hadn't even gotten the photographs yet. She was confused as to how I could possibly have acquired a copy before she did. Apparently we look more similar than either of us had realized, but that photograph made it undeniable. That picture holds so many memories for me, and now I'll always think of that moment Olivia held it in her hand too.

Now both of our sorority composite pictures sit side by side on my desk. I think of them a little differently now. I wonder if my eleven-year-old niece, Gabby, who everyone says looks like a little Olivia, will someday have that same composite picture taken. Will we also see a strong resemblance in her photograph? Will Olivia's children someday compare those photographs to their own?

I imagine those two high school senior pictures that I restored could someday be part of a similar conversation. Maybe even great great grandchildren will look at them and see themselves. They will hold that photo next to their own, and confirm that they share the same grin or narrow jaw line.

Ending Chapter Twelve
Have you made your photographs a priority?

I make a concerted effort to prioritize enjoying photographs with family and friends. Here are ways you can use photographs to connect with loved ones too:

- Make your pictures a conversation starter. I always bring out old photographs at the holidays and anytime we have company. The great memories always start conversations!
- Once you have digital copies of all of your old photographs it is easy to send a thoughtful photo text message or email to an old friend.
- Create photo gifts to share with loved ones. Something as simple as a keychain with a fun old photo can be a most cherished gift.
- Websites like PersonalizationMall.com or shutterfly.com offer options for creating a very unique personalized photo

gift. I also keep my own website up to date with personalized photo gifts that I suggest for every occasion, thekristak.com

- Create a private Facebook page that is intended solely for your closest group to post photo memories. This is a great way to get a blast from the past that only your personal group can see.

- Get creative with photo sharing! My family has a private instagram account that is only used around Christmas time. It is under the name "SantaGram" and is used for family photo trivia in the days leading up to Christmas. I share all sorts of old family pictures along with a family trivia question. From grandparents as children to more recent pictures, I always include the best family memories. The first to answer the question correctly gets a treat. This can get super competitive, especially if you have college kids and the prize is cash sent to their Venmo account!!

CHAPTER THIRTEEN
THE PUBLICITY I DIDN'T ASK FOR

The year was 2007. I was driving to St. Michael Lutheran School to pick up Olivia, when it became abundantly clear, I needed to make some changes.

She was a clever second grader with a silly personality that she maintains to this day. I was a work obsessed mom with zero work/life balance.

I was coming off of one of the best years my business had ever had. We photographed over 150 weddings and countless portraits the year before. My staff had grown and I had purchased the most perfect, industrial chic, 1,500 square foot studio to house my operation. I was likely spread a little thin, but I was determined to also "mom" at full capacity too. That meant leaving my office every day to personally pick up Olivia from school.

I was probably becoming overly confident in my ability to pull it all off or perhaps I just underplayed how hard that really is, but regardless, that all worked fine until the car line incident of 2007.

As I ventured towards the school that day, I began my daily routine. I would stockpile phone messages throughout the day with the intention of returning calls while I was on the drive. Maximizing time, killing two birds with one stone... In my mind I was winning the time management game. So as usual that day, I was making calls as I drove.

Olivia knew this routine well. After I picked her up, she would quietly sit in the backseat and patiently wait for my calls to end. There were clients, other photographers, and networking calls too. There was always a long list of conversations that needed to happen and Olivia would sit in her seat and listen in.

On this day, I pulled up to the school and joined the carline while fully engrossed in a typical, in-depth conversation with a fellow photographer. I could see Olivia in the distance as I slowly made my way forward in the train of cars all waiting to collect their children. As I made it to the pick-up zone, Olivia opened the car door, hopped in, and then closed the door. We got the "go" flag for us to proceed forward, and so we did.

I continued my phone conversation while carefully navigating my way out of the school lot and back on the road home. As usual, I continued on with a conversation that was very important at the time, although now I have no recollection of what it was even about. When I was finally able to break away from the call, I gave Olivia my usual greeting, "Hey, Bean! [a nickname from birth that we lovingly call her to this day] How was school?" But she didn't answer. "Bean?" I said, in a slightly concerned tone.

I tilted my rearview mirror down in an attempt to catch a glimpse of her in the seat behind mine. Sitting where I expected to see my smiling child in her little plaid skort and Lutheran school polo was a lonely black saxophone case.

She did indeed open the door, and she did close the door, but what I thought was her getting in was only her placing her saxophone in the car. She then returned to the sidewalk to get her backpack. I drove away.

There was no child in my car!

I already knew I was never going to be Mom of the Year, but this was ROUGH.

At this point I was 15 minutes away from the school and the car line was over. What was my poor Bean thinking? And how was I going to explain this one to Principal Ziegler?

I rushed back to the school to see no car line and no other students, just a lonely Bean, standing outside with her teacher. The drive around the school that had been overflowing with cars just 30 minutes earlier was now a vacant parking lot. It's mostly a blur of a memory, but I likely approached the school as if I was driving on the Autobahn: airborne, flying over a curb, peeling through the grass to cut the corner.

Olivia, at last, joined her saxophone in the backseat, while the teacher, likely not even wanting to know what had just happened, waved and walked away.

"MOM," she yelled, "Why did you leave me?" I explained, the saxophone, the door shut… She laughed, but while I had successfully turned it into a comedy skit for her enjoyment, I was actually mortified with myself. In my mind, I had just completed the ultimate mom fail.

I made a pact with myself that day, not only was I going to stop talking on the phone when I was picking up Olivia, but I was also going to reevaluate my priorities. My obsession with creating the biggest and best photography empire needed to be curbed.

That year is probably still my best financial year to date, but in retrospect, very far from the best year I've experienced. It was the Great Car Line Incident of 2007, coupled with a few other personal setbacks, that shaped what the next 15 years would look like for me. By prioritizing family, friends, and community, I quickly learned what made life worth living.

As I focused on what was important, where to put my heart, how to spend my time, I also found myself more involved in community service work. Time spent volunteering, often together with Olivia, is much more fulfilling than passing out business cards at a chamber of commerce event. Working to help others in the community has consistently remained important to me and something that I will always prioritize.

It was in this spirit that I looked for ways to help after the hurricane.

While the work I did to restore damaged photographs fit well into my priority list, having my mug splashed all over news stations was exactly something that was not on said list. So much so that at one point, I debated turning down an opportunity to appear on national news. There was so much work to be done and the media was becoming a distraction. Demands to provide images and create new footage of me working was time that was being taken away from helping people. It was just like a phone call that couldn't wait during the car line, only this time I managed to recognize it before it became a problem.

I'm not going to lie though, the media buzz around my work was fun at first. I told my friend Greg, the producer at The Weather Channel, about the work I was doing and he mentioned maybe it was something they would report on sometime. I remember being so excited, I LOVE The Weather Channel. Though it really hadn't occurred to me that what I was doing was "story" worthy.

Southwest Florida, at that time, was "all hands on deck." If you were lucky enough that your home wasn't destroyed, you were helping those that weren't so fortunate. Everyone here, and I mean EVERYONE, has a friend who lost everything. Once you finished helping one person, you moved on to the thousands of others desperate for help. Food banks, water delivery, supply collection, in addition to the many friends I know who did search and rescue; everyone was working hard. My efforts were unique, but not unusual.

Even though Greg saw potential in my story, it actually wasn't The Weather Channel that interviewed me first. I had been posting on social media to get the word out to hurricane victims, letting people know I was available to help and offering tips for drying and cleaning pictures. A local business directory on Instagram, Felipe's Backyard, shared my information. *Good Morning America* had been closely following Felipe's local content and saw my post that he had shared.

Is this a joke? Spam? Those were the first thoughts that went through my head as I saw the email. The subject line read: *"Good Morning America* Interview Request." I had barely wrapped my head around the fact that The Weather Channel might possibly want to talk to me, but now *Good Morning America*? Mind. Blown.

I immediately texted Greg, "OMG YOU WILL NOT BELIEVE THIS."

Greg confirmed what I already knew, *"Good Morning America*, that is huge!"*.

Less than a minute later my phone rang. "Hello, this is Justin Michaels, I'm a reporter with The Weather Channel." I'm not sure how that all went down or what Greg told Justin, but next thing you know I was also lining up an in-person interview with The Weather Channel.

The *Good Morning America* interview was the first to happen a few days later via zoom. I was super nervous but the reporter, Katie Kindelan, made it feel like we were chatting over coffee. I think I likely forgot at one point that it was even a recorded interview, as we got off topic discussing weddings and pets. Fortunately, it was all pre-recorded and successfully clipped down to a short bit that made me look like I do, in fact, know what I'm doing.

Then it all snowballed.

People were reaching out from all over. There were people offering to help with pictures, some who needed help, and there were even more interview requests. It hadn't occurred to me that one interview would lead to so many others, but it did. Fox Weather, NBCLX, several local stations, a couple podcasts, a photography magazine... It really was a daily thing for a couple of weeks.

The Weather Channel was, of course, a highlight. Justin Michaels came to my house with an entire production team. My neighbor, Kaye, joined me for the interview. They wanted to capture the moment where she saw her father's restored photographs for the first time. I don't know if I was even prepared for her reaction. She was literally in tears as she saw the photographs that I had reprinted and spread all across my dining room table. It was dozens of pictures, all reprinted like brand new. Memories from her childhood, family heirlooms, some photographs she forgot she had, all beautifully restored.

Justin Michaels interviewed each of us. I had seen him on TV before but it was a bit surreal to now have him following me through my kitchen as I explained my process. We ended up spending a few hours together, and the crew captured a ton of footage of the work I was doing. Again, that all got clipped down to a short piece but definitely a favorite.

As much as I was enjoying meeting such lovely people and getting my two seconds of TV fame, I was also seeing how that was taking away from the work I was doing. With each interview came requests for specific pictures and extra footage they wanted me to capture. There were pre-interviews and producer meetings. Even just the extra time I spent cleaning my house and blow drying my hair (because the messy bun was not going to cut it on national TV) felt like time away from the mission. My priorities were about helping people, not about being in the spotlight.

I was ready to pull the curtain on my little media moment.

However, a conversation with my college bestie, Jen, and her husband, Ken, made me rethink that. I told them how the media coverage was a bit overwhelming, and I mentioned that I would probably just say no to the next request.

Jen and Ken live many miles away, in Upstate New York. They don't worry too much about hurricanes or storm surges up there, but my work did make them start to think about how painful it would be to lose all of their photographs. My story being repeated on the news had inspired them to start to get digital copies of their pictures and secure all of their old prints.

Ken set up a table in his home office, downloaded a photo scanning app and bought an external hard drive for backing up pictures. He was diligently scanning and saving all of their old photographs, and carefully organizing them on his external hard drive. Jen and Ken told me that my story had inspired them to secure their pictures. They showed me that seeing the tragedy of lost photographs on the news could inspire people everywhere to be proactive and to never have the painful experience of losing their photos.

That was when I started thinking more about the value of inspiring others. Everything I was working on, every damaged photograph, it was all preventable. Maybe that was the true positive to come out of this, not fixing damaged pictures but sharing the tools and inspiration to prevent photographs from ever needing fixing in the first place.

And so my priorities expanded. During those long, mindless hours scanning hurricane-damaged pictures, I was thinking more and more about a larger mission. I was thinking about the person, perhaps many miles away, who was seeing my story on the news and was starting to take action to secure their pictures. I was thinking about the person who might find inspiration in my message. I guess I was thinking about you, really.

So I took the next media opportunity that came my way, with a newfound certainty in my mission. *ABC World News Tonight* with David Muir. Eric, a producer with the show, called me at 10 am offering to feature my story on the 6:30 pm news that same evening. He just needed a long list of footage by 2 pm. As I sat there, still in my pajamas that morning, I wondered how I was going to pull that off in time. Asking someone to bounce around Southwest Florida to get videos of various locations is like asking someone to grab something quick at Costco the week before Christmas. I did my best though, I pulled myself and all of the needed footage together in the nick of time. Sure enough, that evening, as I sat with a group of friends, unsure if they truly would show my story, they did. I'm thinking they must have liked my story because they interviewed me a second time with Miss Toto's class a few months later.

All of that would have been enough media coverage for a normal lifetime, but then came the offer to meet Kelly Clarkson. I'll admit, I likely wouldn't have passed up that opportunity no matter what. I adore Kelly, so the opportunity to chat with her is one I will always take.

There were other interviews after that, but they organically became less time consuming. I didn't feel like I was juggling the interviews with the restoration work any longer. It just fit in here and there. It made sense to me now though. It wasn't the mistake I worried it was. It wasn't like the car line incident. Those interviews really were helping people, only in a different way. It was creating awareness and starting a thought process that was about proactively saving pictures.

Today I get messages everyday from people all across the country who write to thank me for offering the motivation and encouragement they needed to get started securing their pictures. Jen and Ken were right. The media coverage put a spotlight on the risk of having pictures that aren't digitized. It was the publicity I didn't ask for but it did so much more good than I was able to see at the beginning. It was that publicity that led to me talking to you here today.

Ending Chapter Thirteen
Where will you store your digital scans?

My friends Jen and Ken planned ahead and purchased an external hard drive to store their digital photographs. This is a better method than storing pictures on your actual computer. Photo files take up space on a computer and if you collect too many, your computer may begin to operate slower. It's also helpful to have personal photographs all collected and organized in one location, the external hard drive is a great main hub.

How to select an external hard drive for your pictures:

I recommend looking for a 'desktop' hard drive. For added durability, consider a Solid State Drive (SSD). Keep in mind that all hard drives are fragile and have a limited lifespan, so they should always be handled with care.

There are several options for the storage capacity of a hard drive, typically measured in terabytes (TB). The number of photographs a hard drive can hold varies depending on the camera, phone, or scanner used to create the files. Similarly, the file size settings selected in these devices also impact the size of the digital photographs. As a general rule, a 2TB (terabyte) hard drive provides enough storage space for the average personal photo collection.

Additional safe storage options:

I advise everyone to keep photographs stored in multiple places. A hard drive is a great first location, but like any tech product, it can malfunction. I suggest also keeping your photographs in online cloud storage. There are several cloud options that allow you to store any digital scan as well as your cell phone pictures. Many even have options to automatically back up your cell phone so those pictures are always being secured. Cloud storage options include:

Amazon Photos
Dropbox
Google Photos
Microsoft OneDrive
Forever Storage

CHAPTER FOURTEEN
PAINFUL REMINDERS

I was just five years old when I fell in love with photography. A little allowance money and some birthday cash, and by the age of seven I was already annoying my family with my first camera. It was a 126 film camera that looked like a little plastic box. I soon upgraded to my first disc camera, which was probably the biggest mistake of a camera ever created. I'm not sure who thought that a negative the size of your pinky nail would make for a great photograph. A few years later, I entered the big leagues. At fifteen, I was the proud owner of a 35mm manual Vivitar camera with interchangeable lenses, and a fancy camera strap that made me look like I definitely knew what I was doing. That camera would capture many of the Honesdale High School yearbook pictures in the early '90s. It saw me off to college, spent many a late night with me on tedious school projects, and was even there at the first wedding I ever photographed.

My love of photography spans my lifetime, and so I have no shortage of negatives and prints. Most of them are stored in the back of my walk-in bedroom closet, piled high next to shoes I've long forgotten about and winter clothes that have little right to be in South-west Florida. I have kept every old 4x6 print and each negative strip. They mostly all remain in their original pouches, carefully stacked in boxes. I've kept all of them, every single photograph I have taken, every negative too.

I was in my late twenties before I got my first digital camera. At that point I'd already photographed hundreds of weddings and thousands of family portraits, all on film. They were all meticulously stored, each photo numbered, each negative carefully put into a filing system. It was as easy to precisely locate one of my thousands of work negatives as it is to locate a book in the library.

My personal pictures, on the other hand, didn't get the same respect. They were tossed into a box; no numbering, no order, no rhyme, no reason. Some went into albums, but the majority ended up in the same haphazard, systemless pile that stored photos ranging from my childhood neighbor's cat, to my daughter's birth.

Years later, I began to regret not being more organized with my personal pictures. That regret continued on for a few more years before I actually took any action. Every time I would look at those boxes in the furthest corner of my closet I would feel a little disappointment, a little overwhelmed, and considerably frustrated.

Pictures are a part of every single day for me. Yet, somehow, I even found organizing my overwhelming amount of pictures to be daunting. I procrastinated. And then I procrastinated more.

Then one day, amidst a closet cleaning frenzy, I pulled out those boxes. What had started as a brief break to look at old memories, turned into a new project; one with a reinvigorated intent. I began putting my photos in chronological order as I looked at them. It didn't feel like an overwhelming task or a daunting mission. It was simply a fun afternoon looking at pictures. But in starting with that, I had inadvertently begun the process of organizing them.

Once they were all in order, still sitting in boxes on my bedroom floor, I began to think about how challenging the next steps would be. Getting them digitized seemed like a ton of work, even for me. But I decided at that moment, maybe, just maybe, I could finally solve this problem.

I set aside a little time each night. It wasn't a ton of time, just a bit to start scanning the pictures. In just a few weeks I had scanned twenty years of photographs, and it wasn't anywhere near as painful as I had imagined. Once I actually made the time to do it, it was a simple, mindless project.

It's been a few years since I finished sorting and digitizing all of my photos. Today there are so many more scanning methods. There are easy-to-use photo scanners, scanning services, and even apps for phones that do a remarkable job in digitizing pictures. These days, you can scan an entire photo album in minutes with absolutely no technical skills at all.

I think it's easy to procrastinate on a project that you don't know how to start. That was likely the case for so many people I helped. People that wished they had digitized their photographs but had no idea how to do that. I imagine if they had realized how easy it could be, they likely would have digitized their own pictures ages ago.

During the frenzy after Ian, I learned a lot about loss, both preventable and inescapable. Photographs that contained a lost loved one were always the ones that felt the most tragic. One family from Pine Island, Florida already knew the pain of severe loss long before Hurricane Ian's strike. Years ago, they lost their two-year-old daughter. A sweet, young baby girl who would actually be the same age as Olivia if she could be here with us today. I wonder if they would have gone to school together, or if they would have played each other in soccer. Maybe they would have become friends; she would have come to Olivia's birthday parties, or been there for our annual Halloween celebration.

Those things were never a possibility. Instead of meeting that family at the parent pick up line, I met them when they were desperately trying to save their memories of her. That baby girl had her life unexpectedly cut short. The time that family shared with her is remembered through the photographs that they captured, and now they were desperate to save what they could.

The family had created a beautiful memorial album. It was filled with her glowing little smile and all of the wonderful memories they had shared with her. I imagine there were many quiet moments with that album over the years, remembering her.

Twenty years after her passing, Ian struck with its surge of terrible flood water that damaged so much of the area. And with that surge, it took the one thing this family held so dearly—the beautiful memorial album—and destroyed most of it. Those priceless pictures were beaten and stained. Many were so severely damaged you couldn't even tell what they were of.

I understand what it is to have photographs with such infinite value. My own photographs of my late grandmother more than likely influenced much of my own photo journey.

My grandmother was among the many family members that I harassed with my little 126 film camera as a kid. She was never one for having her picture taken. Actually, I don't know if I have even seen many photographs of her from her younger years. She was also the most selfless person there is, happily leaving her comfort zone to accommodate any of her grandchildren's requests. So although she was not eager to be photographed, she would make an exception for me. That typically included me pretending to be a newspaper photographer on an important assignment, the assignment being her. I would interview her, and then capture her photograph, posing her with my cat and a few teddy bears (stand-ins for her co-workers, fellow parishioners at the church, or maybe customers at her store).

Many of the resulting photographs are looking up from the perspective of a not quite four-foot-tall child. Some are blurry and others are awkwardly cropped. Many years would pass before I would hone those skills, but that doesn't diminish the value of those unprofessional photographs. My grandmother was likely my most cooperative subject when I was little. She lived with us, so there was no shortage of opportunities to host some sort of impromptu photo shoot with her, something I took for granted until she passed away when I was eleven years old.

I had been pestering my family with my camera for years at that point, but it was never with any thought that someday those photos would be the only tangible memories I could hold. I remember after my grandmother's passing, I went through all of my stacks of photographs and set aside all of the pictures of her. I kept them in a little box by my bed. My grandmother and I were very close, and those pictures held our memories. I learned then, at eleven years old, the power of a photograph.

I have carried that knowledge with me both in my personal photography, and my career as a photographer. With every photograph I take, I know there is the possibility that someday it could be the one remaining memory of a loved one whom we can no longer hug.

As I helped the family to save their photographs of their little baby girl, I thought a lot about the pictures I still keep of my grandmother. It's been well over thirty years since her passing, but it's those pictures that keep her with me to this day. Photographs do keep the memories alive.

I was determined to keep the memories of that baby girl alive. Many of the photographs were unrecognizable; the muddy salt water had destroyed them. But that only made saving the ones I could that much more imperative. I know every volunteer involved in fixing those pictures was equally as determined. In the end, we were able to completely restore about 25% of them. When I returned the photographs to the family I was concerned about disappointment, since so many couldn't be saved. Instead I was met with tears of joy. They later said they had hoped I would be able to save one or two. The fact that dozens were brought back to life was far beyond their expectations.

Now with every heartbreaking story of lost photographs, I find more and more motivation to encourage everyone to proactively secure their pictures. It isn't just natural disasters or fluke occurrences that destroy pictures, it's also our own lack of proper organization with our photographs. All of our photographs. The old ones, the new ones, the quantity, the mess. And that mess just builds with time and more pictures. Though the prospect of getting organized is inevitably daunting, it really is worth the effort, more than any of us even realize.

Ending Chapter Fourteen
Inheriting old photographs

Having old photographs of late loved ones is so important, but often with the passing of a loved one comes the decades of old photographs that are passed down. One of the most common situations I'm asked to help with is organizing an enormous group of pictures that has been inherited. There are a few steps I suggest everyone take when in that situation.

Steps to organize inherited photographs

- Begin looking through the photographs and start the process by putting them in chronological order.
- If you need to narrow down the collection, separate out the valuable photographs. Your grandparents' honeymoon trip to the Grand Canyon may include dozens of scenic snapshots that may not interest you, but mixed in may be special ones of the two of them. Identify those that are significant to your family and eliminate those that are not ones you wish to carry on.
- Talk to family members to identify people and places in photographs where it is not noted. Make sure to note names of people and places and add dates where you can now. This information will be harder and harder to gather as time goes on.
- Begin to get digital scans of all of the photographs. Apps like Photomyne will allow you to quickly scan groups of photographs and will also colorize old black-and-white images. An at-home scanner is also an easy option. I suggest the Epson FastFoto scanner.
- Old photo albums with outdated covers or pages that are not archival quality can be taken apart and the photographs can be put into new albums. Taking this step means those pictures are more apt to be viewed and enjoyed now.
- Add important family photographs to a heritage folder.

- Create a memorial album of your late loved one and share it with family members. Digital album services like Chatbooks or Simple Prints make it easy to design an album and affordably produce duplicate copies for everyone in the family. For a higher-quality option, photo labs like Printique offer digital photo albums with exceptional printing. These are designed to stand the test of time, providing a lasting tribute to your loved one.

CHAPTER FIFTEEN
PICTURES TODAY

I t's a popular aspiration to want to one day write a book and share one's story... As I began this journey, I would frequently be asked about my "dream of writing a book."

This was never my dream. My world has always been about photography. It very literally never crossed my mind to write a book. However, as I realized how many people have not taken the easy steps to prevent the heartache of lost pictures, I felt the need to share this story.

Helping people with flood-damaged photographs and seeing their anguish over lost pictures was definitely the catalyst. It was all so preventable. Getting the information in the hands of more people to prevent them from ever having to feel what is truly unnecessary pain, that is my vision.

So here we are together, in chapter fifteen of my book.

Since the moment I began typing, my mind has been fixated on offering solutions to all of our photo organization woes. Over the course of a few months, I took a deep dive into figuring out exactly how organized most people are. I asked everyone: friends, family, Uber drivers, bartenders, Publix cashiers. Everyone I spoke with: "Where do your photographs live?"

The vast majority of people don't have a digital backup of their older print photographs. After my experience post Ian, I can't say I was surprised. I was, however, surprised at how many people mentioned having had old photographs lost or destroyed. Pictures lost in a move, an only copy misplaced, damage from the sun, mold, humidity. The damage done far exceeded the hurricane.

A few of the people I spoke with I then coached on how they could digitally back up their photographs. Even the least tech-savvy person would tell me how easy it was. Interestingly, I found the hardest part for most people was just setting aside a little time.

One of the individuals I talked with was my friend Rhonda. Rhonda's son's home was flooded during the hurricane. He had incurred a lot of home damage and Rhonda was seeing first hand how quickly and easily things can be destroyed. Now she was motivated to get her own pictures digitized and safely secured.

Rhonda invited me to her home to look at the photographs she had. When I arrived, she had already pulled out all of her old photo albums. A dozen or so colorful books filled with old pictures were all spread across her bed.

Our goal was to create a secure backup for all of those photographs, as well as organize them into a digital collection that she could easily share with her now grown daughter and son.

I quickly made myself at home, grabbed an album, and sat down crisscrossed on her living room floor. As I leafed through the pages of her old albums, I could see some were already becoming discolored. Those pictures went back over thirty years, of course they were showing signs of aging.

Identifying and organizing was the first step. Somehow that always seems like it would be the most tedious part, but honestly, it's the most fun. It's the step that includes reminiscing and talking about old memories.

Rhonda poured us each a glass of wine, and we continued to look through her memories. A photo of her as a child and one of her daughter baking a cake; it was sweet to look at her old pictures together. We laughed about some funny moments, the "slightly" dated outfits, and how she had way too many photographs of squirrels.

Once those albums were all in chronological order and each photo was removed, I helped Rhonda with scanning each photo. We downloaded a photo scanning app to her phone. We then found a bright, well-lit corner near the sliding glass doors that led out to her patio. From there we began scanning each of the large oversized pictures, as well as the ones that were most fragile.

We then used my Epson FastFoto scanner to quickly zip through the piles of photographs she had created from each of her albums. That scanner is perfect for digitizing stacks of 4x6 sized pictures because it has a feeder that automatically sends through and scans each pile of pictures. In addition to quickly capturing scans, it also has software that will correct the colors in old photographs. It gave new life to some of Rhonda's oldest pictures and even brightened up pictures from as recent as the early 2000s.

A couple of glasses of wine later, and we had already checked off a good part of the project. By the time I left that day, the majority of the project was done, and she had an easy game plan to finish the work. Within a week or so, she had completely finished the job. She not only organized folders on her computer, she was also able to share those pictures with her kids.

That one day spent with Rhonda has actually led to many more fun photo-digitizing days with friends. I've learned that digitizing pictures with a group is actually a really good time. As I've mentioned before, I can definitely turn anything into a party, but I think this activity has some serious merit.

Now, I wholeheartedly encourage everyone to do it! Gather your friends and ask each to bring a couple of photo albums. Aside from that, a few bottles of wine (optional), and a photo scanning app will get the group started. Go around the room and ask everyone to share pictures. Who has the oldest photo? Who has the funniest photo? Most embarrassing? The stories are the best part. However, helping each other to get the ball rolling on scanning is the goal. Just like any daunting project, the hardest part is getting started.

Which brings me to another seemingly overwhelming task I've often heard in conversation: phone pictures. Years of unorganized pictures, uncertainty about how to back them up, and accidentally deleted images are common complaints. I was hearing similar struggles repeatedly, and it's become evident that unorganized digital pictures are a common problem.

Most people I've spoken with have digital pictures that would stretch a mile long. Fun fact: 10,560 4x6 prints lined up end to end would actually stretch a mile. I think it's okay to have miles of photographs. I'm not here to tell you to start deleting things. Though don't get me wrong, I do think the photo of where you parked at the airport likely can go. But when you have an organized system, making decisions about what can be deleted becomes easier. I encourage everyone to separate the important moments from the screenshots and less flattering selfies, and then you can make choices as to what needs to be discarded.

59,188. That is the exact amount of pictures on my phone right now. If printed, that would be 5.6 miles, to be exact. That might seem like a lot to keep organized, but believe it or not, they are in a very organized system. They are backed up online and on an external hard drive too. I have them categorized in folders, and I always note my favorites. Each month, I print a very small group of those favorites, sometimes as few as 25 pictures. Just enough to highlight that month. I place those 4x6 prints in a running album, which, by the end of the year, tells a beautiful story. It sits on our coffee table, and everyone that comes to my home picks it up. It contains just the right amount of pictures that make for an interesting story of our family, rather than an overwhelming behemoth.

Maintaining smaller, more manageable groups of images is especially great when you want to show friends the pictures on your phone. I can tell a friend about our trip to Antigua without leafing through every meal we ate while we were there. It's quick, it's easy, and it really takes minimal effort to do.

When we significantly narrow down our collection of pictures, they become interesting again. I like to imagine that my grandchildren will someday be interested in the story I've curated in each smaller photo album. They are like the box of treasures my mother kept with my own childhood pictures. An interesting collection, not overwhelming, but just enough to be enjoyable to view.

My 96-year-old mother-in-law, Kit, has six albums that sit on a side table in her living room. 96 years narrowed down to a few albums, totaling maybe 1,500 pictures. Whenever we visit, someone always picks them up, and Kit will always give background details as we look through them. Each photo holds a story. There is a photograph of her dressed in an '80s power suit, standing in front of the high rise building she worked at in San Francisco. With that photo always comes stories of co-workers, business deals, and how much she enjoyed grabbing lunch by the fountain. A candid childhood moment of my husband and his brothers at the family's annual St. Patrick's Day party will inevitably lead to the story of that night's shenanigans and the trouble those four boys found themselves in.

If I live to be 96, I want shareable stories too. I want to show my grandchildren the photo of their mom's fifth birthday party and explain how we were all singing along to Gwen Stefani's "Hollaback Girl," Olivia's favorite song at that time. That will inevitably lead to the story of how a line from the song led to her learning how to spell her first word, B-A-N-A-N-A-S, and how she would insist it was played on repeat for a solid six months. And, of course, we will laugh as I share how that drove us, "bananas."

A photo of my father, Grandpa Frank, on his Christmas tree farm will spark conversations about generations of green thumbs, a passion I know goes all the way back to my grandparents in Poland. I loved seeing the old black-and-white photographs of their farm. Would I have even known that they were expert gardeners if it weren't for the pictures that held those stories? Will future generations share that same interest? Will the photographs inspire them to explore gardening too?

I wouldn't be able to share these moments, the same way Kit has, if I wasn't organized with my pictures now. Photos left unorganized could mean trying to show grandchildren a million pictures or even more. At the rate I'm taking cell phone pictures, when I turn 95 I will have over two million personal pictures. Two million! That fifth birthday photo would disappear amongst screenshots of my high score at Words With Friends and a photo of the questionable freckle on my calf.

Instead, my important photographs are organized in folders on my computer *and* printed out. They are special, and I've treated them that way. This is the manageable group that will be talked about.

I think it's important to our heritage that we take these steps now. It's our history and the stories of our lives. And taking the time and effort to curate those stories, will make them all the more accessible for generations to come.

As important as heritage and legacy are, it is equally important that we preserve our memories for ourselves. And it's pictures that keep our memories alive. Whether passed down or not, some photographs are simply for oneself and the emotions they evoke.

Keeping old print photographs and recent digital phone pictures neatly organized in the same location isn't impossible. It's a very manageable task, but it's a new task. It's not a task our parents and grandparents had to tackle. Back in 1980, when I imagine the average family used up four rolls of film a year, they could wait five years before organizing pictures and it was still manageable. Now people are taking what was then the equivalent of five years of photographs in any single month. And the issue only compounds itself as we increasingly use photos as shorthand for everything from remembering where we parked to getting a second opinion on a new haircut. All to say, the special moments and memories can get lost in the shuffle now more than ever before.

Securing your pictures is the only thing that will protect them from a hurricane or natural disaster. It's also what will protect your photographs from just becoming lost in a sea of useless digital files. Taking the necessary steps today to pull all of your pictures together in one organized group is the solution. It's a project you'll appreciate taking on, and one that your family will appreciate for generations to come.

Ending Chapter Fifteen
How to secure and organize your most recent photographs

Today we are adding photographs to our collections at a record pace. It's just as important to keep your phone photographs organized too.

Tips for organizing and securing phone pictures

- Everyday or once a week set aside a moment to look at your most recent phone pictures. Most days it will likely only take a minute but make it a habit to look at your pictures as often as you can.
- Click on the heart icon to signify the ones that are your favorites.
- Delete unwanted photographs. In the photo albums on most phones, there is the option to solely select screenshots in the albums. You can also select duplicates. Start by looking at those and eliminating those unneeded screenshots and duplicate photographs.
- There are also apps like Daily Delete that will automatically sort photographs on your phone. Daily Delete will identify both the pictures that it thinks are "the best," but also will suggest pictures to eliminate. You can view its choices and correct its work. It then uses AI to learn your preferences and become better at the process.
- Once a month print 4x6 pictures. I suggest using a photo lab with an easy app to order right from your phone. I do an annual photo lab comparison where I order prints from several photo labs and list the pros and cons of each lab. If you are just starting out, this is a great resource that you can use to help you select a photo lab that is best for you. You can access that information through my website.
- Once you've decided on a photo lab, select images from your "favorites" group. That group can even be narrowed down further, if needed. Even just printing 25 pictures per month

of the most important photographs gives you and your family the opportunity to enjoy them.

- Keep a running photo album and add your pictures to that album each month. Leave that album out for family and friends to peruse.
- Select the photographs that you want to add to a heritage folder.
- Back up those photographs. Save your phone pictures to a cloud service like Amazon Photos or Google Photos. They should also be backed up to your computer, preferably on an external hard drive. This is an easy task if you do it monthly.

CHAPTER SIXTEEN
WHAT'S NEXT?

Back in 1997, when I was cruising around Fort Myers in my little red stick-shift Mazda as a new Floridian, I never would have imagined all of the places life would take me. Moving to Florida was one of the wisest decisions I've ever made. It's shaped who I've become and allowed me the photography career that five-year-old me had only dreamed of.

My little business, Impressions Photography, bloomed quickly in the Florida sunshine. Over the years, it's served me well. Opportunities I likely would have never had, had I stayed in rural Pennsylvania or even Upstate New York after college, came my way because I pursued my photography dream in Florida.

Now, years later, I've photographed around 1,500 weddings and thousands of families. Photography has taken me from the sidelines of the Tampa Bay Buccaneers football games to private jets cruising around the country. My work has made the cover of magazines, it's been on billboards, it's won awards. All because I decided to make a go of it in Florida.

Photography is like a best friend that goes all the way back to preschool for me; the one you've known so long you don't even recall how you were introduced, you just know your life would be incomplete without them. My life story couldn't be told without photography being woven into almost every sentence.

I thought my journey was full and complete long before Hurricane Ian. I didn't have the vision to see how photography could play yet another role in my story. However, as I share the significance of preserving, maintaining, and restoring an organized photo collection, I'm struck with the same passion I feel when I have a camera in my hand.

Mother Nature wasn't the kindest to us here in Southwest Florida. I wish it were under different circumstances that I ventured on this photo-organizing mission. There are so many moments of these past years I would love to simply wish away. However, preventing others from ever experiencing the pain that I witnessed from so many over lost photos, has proven to be nothing short of a silver lining.

Truth is, I can't wish those terrible months away. At best, I can only wait as they gradually transform into distant memories. In what felt like the blink of an eye, a new hurricane season came and went. I wish I could report that life all went back to normal and everything was like new again, but Hurricane Ian's impact was and is still seen and felt throughout Southwest Florida.

It was a full year before I found the courage (and had the need) to cross back over the bridge to Fort Myers Beach. I had made that trip so frequently for over twenty years; I didn't want to face what would lie on the other side of the bridge. There was land still piled with debris and rubble where houses and businesses used to stand. I would hear stories of people living in condemned homes that had only further dilapidated since the storm. Work fences and caution tape surrounded buildings that barely stood.

The storm itself is said to have taken 160 lives. I imagine that number is so much higher when you consider the events in the days, months and years after the storm. Weeks without utilities and a treacherous clean up had to have had a deadly impact on some. Not to mention the potentially unbearable mental and emotional toll of losing so much so suddenly. Driving over to Fort Myers Beach, seeing the still-present painful reminders of such tragedy, was something I had understandably avoided till then.

But recovery does happen. Albeit slowly, things can and do get better. One year after the hurricane, only two of the sixty island restaurants had reopened with indoor seating. However, there has been progress since. With each passing week another one opens, adding to the list of new eateries. Some chose to rebuild, others are brand new. Another dozen or so food trucks are set up on vacant lots where restaurants once sat. Cafe lights, picnic tables and freshly painted murals surround those outdoor spots, offering even makeshift locations some classic island charm. Each one sits within earshot of the gentle waves of the Gulf of Mexico. Even the most rustic of set ups have the kind of ambiance that Jimmy Buffet could have written a song about.

Sanibel Island is also on a slow path to recovery. Seventy years of old Florida charm at Castaway Beach Cottages now remains a vacant lot. The sixty-year-old island staple, Bailey's General Store, also demolished. I imagine both will return with fresh new buildings, but that isn't the case for others. My friend Jana's flower shop, which thrived for 25 years, has permanently closed its doors at its island location. Other buildings still stand, but with severe damage and a lot of work still ahead. The Bubble Room, Casa Ybel Resort, The Colony Inn, as of now, not a one has even announced a possible reopening date. The vegetation has begun to fill back in and the debris has all been removed from the sides of the streets, but even today you don't have to look hard to see the hurricane's impact. Many of the old beach front condos sit vacant, some in the midst of a slow recovery, others completely untouched since the storm. Insurance struggles, financing, and government red tape have made rebuilds a challenge, but little by little, each one is finding its way to joining the group of revitalized buildings.

Beach weddings, some more than a year post hurricane, continue to be rescheduled and relocated. Instead of a commute over the Sanibel Island Causeway, there have been many long hauls up I-75 or across Alligator Alley to Miami, and down to the Florida Keys, to get to relocated weddings. I've racked up hotel points, spending weekends far from home, in order to keep the few photography contracts that I still have. As those wedding dates pass, few new events join my calendar.

The Southwest Florida wedding industry continues to see hardship. However, with each day comes news of new and improved additions to our once vibrant tourist industry. I am optimistic that in 2025 we will see a resurgence in destination weddings. The area has already regained its beloved natural charm. Now that it is adding to it some of the newest and most updated hotels and wedding venues in the entire state of Florida, I think it will inevitably be among the top destinations in the country.

There have been great strides to welcome back all tourists. Hotels that have been able to reopen boast many nights with full occupancy, proving that the beauty of the region already outshines the destruction. New and grand properties like the Margaritaville Resort are welcoming even more guests to the area, and proposed luxury hotels and upscale shopping areas might just be the draw our beach communities need. With each new announcement, it's already obvious this region is on track to once more reign as a sought after vacation destination.

Even now, while the recovery is still in progress, traffic is clearly making its comeback, a sign that tourists are already here in full force. While that isn't something any local would normally be excited about, it is a good sign. A great number of local residents work in or are impacted by tourism. It is a key part of our recovery.

Although many residents are returning to their tourism jobs, there are still a great number that are out of work or are waiting for their jobs to come back. Like the impact the hurricane had on my business, there has been a financial impact on almost everyone that I know. From lost wages to insurance deductibles, to insurance just refusing to pay, very few residents got away unscathed.

Multiple families sharing a single home, insurance claims denied, FEMA slow to assist and government agencies offering no help, are challenges many people still face. However, as time passes, the tragedy of Hurricane Ian is becoming a forgotten story for many people outside of Southwest Florida.

Just days ago, Maddie and I traveled up to Clearwater, Florida, to photograph a relocated wedding. A short two-and-a-half-hour drive up the coast, but far enough that we met people who were unaware of what Southwest Florida is still up against. A waitress we encountered said, "Oh yeah, I guess I heard you had some flooding down there," struggling to understand why the wedding had been relocated to Clearwater.

A soaring homeless population, with people living in cars, RVs, and tents, as well as thousands of homes and businesses still uninhabitable; many outside the area don't know the havoc the hurricane still wreaks. Sometimes, the things that aren't in our own backyard fade from our minds when the news crews leave.

My own story, helping hurricane victims, has become old news too. The time when it was relevant to news stations has passed, but I hope that what can be learned from my experience will continue to impact people everywhere. There is a takeaway from this story, something that I hope will change the trajectory of many peoples' own photographs. The motivation to take the next steps, the inspiration to get organized, the decision to be proactive—those are still very pertinent and important sentiments.

This story, the one about saving hurricane-damaged photographs, has been told. The work has been done. However, unorganized photographs, pictures that are not secured or backed up, and overwhelming quantities of digital pictures; that is a problem in its infancy. That story is just beginning to unfold and be told.

I've continued on helping people with their pictures. Now, It's all about being proactive. Scott was relieved to see the dining room table finally cleared. The bar cart, once used as my digital-photo scanning station, has been returned to its original use. I threw out those yellow dish gloves. There haven't been negatives strung across the kitchen, or plastic tubs set up as makeshift sinks in a long time, but I'm still talking to people about their photographs everyday.

Today, I'm focused on guiding and assisting others as I help people proactively organize their photographs. I host workshops, I teach classes and I offer tips on social media. I like this new mission a lot better. There are no tears, no heart-breaking stories of survival keeping me up at night. Now, my conversations are fun and hope-filled.

People still share with me how much value a particular photograph holds. They still tell me about pictures they would be lost without.

"Their most valued possession," I still hear. And I too still pause and think of the power each one holds.

It was the power of photography that captured my heart when I was just five years old. The power of a photograph has kept memories of my grandmother alive, made me laugh over an old sorority photo with my daughter, and brought countless others to tears when a photograph they thought was ruined was returned to them like new. I have been moved by the power of photographs, and I am certain you have been too.

My hope is that this serves as a reminder for all, that such a powerful object requires love and care.

Within our grasp lies the power to make change in the course of our own photo legacy, in the memories we carry forward. We hold the power to shape what our grandchildren will see of us, what will be remembered of us. Will it be the photos of your significant moments and biggest achievements? Or will it be photos of meaningless paperwork and parking tickets?

This story may belong to Lori, Denise, Kaye, her father, myself, and many other Southwest Florida residents. Yet, it could belong to anyone. It could be yours. Lost and damaged photographs extend far beyond my region and a storm. They can happen to anyone. But they don't have to.

Where do your photographs live now?

How will you safeguard the most tangible form of your memories?

Ending Chapter Sixteen
Keep the photo organizing momentum going!

Do you need more inspiration? Follow along on Instagram @The.Krista.K and on Facebook @TheKristaK for daily photo organizing tips. You can also join the photo organizing community at www.TheKristaK.com and receive monthly emails with even more tips and tricks to always keep your photographs safe and secure!

Resources

Links to recommended products, upcoming photo organizing workshops and behind the scenes photos from Beyond The Storm.

www.TheKristaK.com/Beyond-The-Storm

REFERENCES

Powell, Emily. "Florida Climate Center" 11/14/22
https://climatecenter.fsu.edu/images/docs/Hurri
cane_Ian_Report.pdf

Oliveri, Zach. "Wink News" 5/16/23
https://winknews.com/2023/03/15/messed-up-traffic-
lights-frustrating-drivers-across-lee-county-after-hurricane-ian/
Hurricane Ian had caused over $100 billion in damages

Rafferty, John P. "Britannica" 8/20/24
https://www.britannica.com/event/Hurricane-Ian-2022

Shipley, Andrew "Fox 4 NOW" 1/11/23
https://www.fox4now.com/news/local-news/hurricane-
ian-ranks-as-the-costliest-natural-disaster-in-usa-during-2022

Green, Amy. "Inside Climate News" 9/28/23
https://insideclimatenews.org/news/28092023/sanibel-
recovery-from-hurricane-ian-years-in-the-making/

Staff "Sanibel Captiva Island, Reporter, Islander & Current" 10/2/23

https://www.captivasanibel.com/2023/10/02/one-year-since-hurricane-ian-hit/

"FEMA" 3/8/23

https://www.fema.gov/fact-sheet/hurricane-ian-response-and-recovery

Raia, James. "Gulfshore Business" 12/1/22

https://www.gulfshorebusiness.com/finding-replacement-vehicles-after-hurricane-ian/